CW00421938

OLIVE SCHREINER

WW

OLIVE
SCHREINER

Carolyn Burdett

© Copyright 2013 by Carolyn Burdett

First published in 2013 by Northcote House Publishers Ltd, Horndon, Tavistock, Devon, PL19 9NQ, United Kingdom.
Tel: +44 (0) 1822 810066 Fax: +44 (0) 1822 810034.

British Library Cataloguing-in-Publication Data
A catalogue record for this book is available from the British Library

ISBN 978-0-7463-1088-5 hardcover
ISBN 978-0-7463-1093-9 paperback

Typeset by PDQ Typesetting, Newcastle-under-Lyme
Printed and bound in the United Kingdom

For Dinah Birch

Contents

Acknowledgements

My thanks to Angelique Richardson for reading and commenting on a full draft. Ella Dzelzainis and Lawrence Normand were my imagined and real 'Writers and their Work' readers and I thank them for bearing with the task and for some phrases that they'll recognize here, for which I'm very grateful.

Biographical Outline

1855   24 March, born Olive Emily Albertina, ninth child of Gottlob Schreiner and Rebecca Lyndall, on the Wittebergen mission station in Basutoland.

1861–6   Family move to Healdtown; Schreiner's Wesleyan education provided by her mother.

1867   Gottlob becomes insolvent; the family disperses, and Schreiner moves to live with siblings, beginning a pattern of frequent movement.

1868–70   Moves to Cradock in the Karoo with a brother and sister, making use of its lending library.

1871–2   Lives in Dordrecht; begins to read Darwin, Mill and others; possible love affair with Julius Gau to whom she is briefly engaged. Begins to suffer the asthma-related symptoms which trouble her throughout her life.

1872–3   Moves to the Diamond Fields (Kimberley); begins *Undine*. Meets Mary and John Brown who offer support and encouragement over the next years.

1874–80   Works as a governess, serving a series of families in the Karoo region. Writes *The Story of an African Farm* and *From Man to Man*.

1881   Leaves South Africa for England, initially with plans to pursue a medical training which are swiftly abandoned because of poor health.

1882   Meets Eleanor Marx; becomes involved in socialist debates.

1883   *The Story of an African Farm* published in two volumes by Chapman & Hall.

1884   Meets Havelock Ellis, and begins a lifelong friendship and correspondence; attends the Fellowship of the New Life; meets Edward Carpenter.

1885–6	Attends the Men and Women's Club and meets Karl Pearson. Her asthma treated by the Marx family doctor, Horatio Bryan Donkin, who proposes to her several times.
1886	Conceives a plan for a non-fictional 'sex book'. Relationship with Pearson breaks down, and Schreiner suffers physical and mental collapse. Moves to the continent.
1887–9	Lives mainly in Italy, writes allegories, works on *From Man to Man*, and begins an (unfinished) introduction to Mary Wollstonecraft's *Vindication of the Rights of Woman*.
1889	Returns to South Africa, initially living in Cape Town. Her brother, William Philip, already a prominent figure in Cape politics.
1890	Moves to Matjesfontein in the Karoo region of the Cape. Begins essays on South Africa and Boer life eventually collected as *Thoughts on South Africa*; meets Cecil Rhodes. *Dreams* published.
1891	Writes stories and a skit on the Cape Parliament's debate of the Masters and Servants Bill which sanctioned the use of the lash on Africans.
1892	Ends friendship with Rhodes; meets a young farmer, Samuel Cron Cronwright.
1893	*Dream Life and Real Life*, a collection of three short stories, published. W. P. Schreiner appointed Attorney-General in Rhodes's Second Ministry.
1894	Marries Cronwright who agrees to take her name. They live on his farm until her worsening asthma necessitates a move to Kimberley.
1895	Birth and death of Schreiner's only child. Cronwright delivers a public address on 'The Political Situation', a critique of monopolistic capitalism, co-authored with Schreiner.
1896	*The Political Situation* published. Jameson Raid forces Rhodes' resignation as Prime Minister, and W. P. Schreiner breaks with Rhodes. The South African Chartered Company's actions in Mashonaland and Matabeleland inspire *Trooper Peter Halket of Mashonaland* which explicitly attacks Rhodes.
1897	Travels to England to publish *Trooper Peter*.

1898   Moves to Johannesburg for her health; Cronwright gives up his business and joins her; W. P. Schreiner becomes Prime Minister of the Cape.

1899   Writes *An English South African's View of the Situation*. *Words in Season*. Leaves Johannesburg for Cape Town on the eve of war which breaks out in November. 'The Woman Question' published in two parts in the New York *Cosmopolitan*, and is later incorporated in *Woman and Labour*.

1900   Lives in Hanover under martial law restrictions.

1902   Works on *Woman and Labour*, and stories, including 'Eighteen-Ninety-Nine'. Peace treaty signed; visits Johannesburg and her looted house. In the years following the war Schreiner and Cronwright spend much of the time apart.

1905   Letter to the Johannesburg Shop Assistants' Union argues for international unionism across the colour bar.

1906   Publishes 'A Letter on the Jew', which condemns antisemitism.

1907   Moves from Hanover to De Aar, where Cronwright had established a business, though Schreiner spends parts of the year in Cape Town or Matjesfontein.

1908   Involved in public debate about the future South African constitution. Joins the Women's Enfranchisement League as vice-president, later resigning when its policy changes to exclude non-white women.

1909   *Closer Union* published, advocating federation against union. Meets Gandhi and becomes a supporter of his *satyagraha* movement.

1911   *Woman and Labour* published. Schreiner lobbies against racist attitudes in the 'Black Peril' investigations.

1913   Leaves South Africa for Europe, seeking treatment for her heart condition. In London at the end of the year, meets old friends including Ellis, Carpenter, Constance Lytton, and Adela Villiers Smith.

1914   War declared. Schreiner spends the war years in England, in contact with pacifists and conscientious objectors. Her health is poor.

1916	Address on 'Conscientious Objectors' for the *Labour Leader*; participates in deputation to the Commons to lobby against conscription; supports equal pay for women taking men's jobs.
1917	A work on pacifism, 'Who Knocks at the Door?', published in the *Fortnightly Review*. Begins a book about war.
1920	Cronwright visits Schreiner in London, and is shocked by her physical deterioration. She returns to South Africa in August. Dies of heart failure during the night of 10–11 December at a boarding house in Wynberg, a suburb of Cape Town.
1921	The bodies of Olive Schreiner, her baby daughter, and her favourite dog reinterred in a stone sarcophagus on the top of Buffels Kop, in the Karoo. *The Dawn of Civilization*, a fragment from Schreiner's book on war, published in the *Nation and Atheneum*.
1923	*Stories, Dreams and Allegories*, a collection of Schreiner's as yet unprinted fiction, and *Thoughts on South Africa* published.
1924	Cronwright's *Life* and *Letters* published.
1926	*From Man to Man* published.
1929	*Undine* published.

Abbreviations

CU	*Closer Union: A Letter on the South African Union and the Principles of Government* (London: Fifield, 1909)
D.	*Dreams* (2nd edn; London: Unwin, 1891)
DLRL	*Dream Life and Real Life: A Little African Story* (London: Unwin, 1893)
ESAV	*An English-South African's View of the Situation: Words in Season* (London: Stodder & Houghton, 1899)
FMM	*From Man to Man* (London: Virago, 1982)
LiOS	*The Life of Olive Schreiner*, S. C. Cronwright-Schreiner, (London: Unwin, 1924)
LOS	*The Letters of Olive Schreiner 1876–1920*, ed. S. C. Cronwright-Schreiner (London: Unwin, 1924)
MOS	*My Other Self: the Letters of Olive Schreiner and Havelock Ellis, 1884–1920*, ed. Yaffa Claire Draznin (New York: Peter Lang, 1992)
OALH	*Only an Anguish to Live Here: Olive Schreiner and the Anglo-Boer War 1899–1902*, Karel Shoeman (Cape Town and Johannesburg: Human and Rousseau, 1992)
OSB	*Olive Schreiner: A Biography*, Ruth First and Ann Scott (London: Andre Deutsch, 1980)
OSL	*Olive Schreiner Letters Volume 1: 1871–1899*, ed. Richard Rive (Oxford: Oxford University Press, 1988)
PS	*The Political Situation*, Olive Schreiner and S. C. Cronwright-Schreiner (London: Unwin, 1896)
SAF	*The Story of an African Farm* (Oxford: Oxford University Press, 1992)
SDA	*Stories, Dreams and Allegories* (London: Unwin, 1923)
TPH	*Trooper Peter Halket of Mashonaland* (Parklands: AD. Donker, 1992)
TSA	*Thoughts on South Africa* (Parklands: AD. Donker, 1992)
U.	*Undine* (New York and London: Harper, 1929)

WL   *Woman and Labour* (London: Virago, 1978)
WSA   *Olive Schreiner: A Woman in South Africa 1855–1881*, Karel
      Schoeman (Johannesburg: Jonathan Ball, 1991)

Introduction

In April 1883, the curmudgeonly *Saturday Review* performed a hatchet-job on what it judged 'a clever, imaginative, original, and terribly dull' recently published novel. It was called *The Story of an African Farm*, and the reviewer lamented that while the title might lead a reader to expect 'adventure on the borderland between savagery and civilization', in fact the story was a mix of questionable morals and wayward plotting.[1] Many readers, however, disagreed, and within a few months of first appearing it was sold out and a second edition being prepared. 'Ralph Iron', the name on the title page, was soon discovered to be the pseudonym of a young woman from South Africa called Olive Schreiner, and the novel made her a literary celebrity.

The second edition of *The Story of an African Farm* contained a Preface by the author which in part responded to the *Saturday Review*'s comments. Acknowledging that some readers were puzzled by a novel where some characters appear only fleetingly, yet seem important, Schreiner notes that 'Human life may be painted according to two methods':

> There is the stage method. According to that each character is duly marshalled at first, and ticketed; we know with an immutable certainty that at the right crises each one will reappear and act his part, and, when the curtain falls, all will stand before it bowing. There is a sense of satisfaction in this, and of completeness. But there is another method – the method of the life we all lead. Here nothing can be prophesied. There is a strange coming and going of feet. Men appear, act and re-act upon each other, and pass away. When the crisis comes the man who would fit it does not return. When the curtain falls no one is ready. When the footlights are brightest they are blown out; and what the name of the play is no one knows.... Life may be painted according to either method; but the methods are

1

different. The canons of criticism that bear upon the one cut cruelly upon the other. (*SAF* 27)

The different kind of realism advocated here is explicitly associated with the author's colonial identity. 'Ralph Iron' could not write the African adventure stories featuring 'hair-breadth escapes' that the *Saturday Review* preferred: those stories are the stuff of metropolitan imaginations and 'are best written in the Piccadilly or in the Strand'. As a woman and a colonial, Schreiner was striving for a literary style and form adequate to her distinctive experience: 'should one sit down to paint the scenes' of one's own environment, then the facts necessarily creep in. 'Sadly [the author] must squeeze the colour from his brush', Schreiner went on, 'and dip it into the grey pigments around him. He must paint what lies before him' (*SAF* 28). In fact this apparently realist manifesto initiates a lifelong and often restless engagement with a wide variety of literary forms. This book examines how Schreiner's experiments with literary tradition were an integral part of her political activism and, at the same time, central to her exploration of identity and selfhood. Writing was both intensely private and personal ('I write for myself and to myself' (*OSL* 148)) and thoroughly public and political. For Schreiner, writing helped give shape to ideas of process and change, and thus create the indispensible quality of hope on which politics and self both depend.

Olive Emily[2] Albertina Schreiner was born on 24 March 1855 at Wittebergen, Basutoland (now Lesotho), in South Africa's Cape Colony. She was the ninth of twelve children, five of whom died in infancy (Schreiner's given names come from three dead brothers). Her German father and English mother, Gottlob and Rebecca, had travelled from England to South Africa to become missionaries at the end of 1837. For the next thirty years they worked on mission stations in more or less isolated regions of the Cape Colony, where living conditions were often difficult and perilous. Colonial expansion periodically triggered wars with indigenous African peoples, occasionally threatening the safety of the family. By the end of the nineteenth century, South Africa had undergone profound transformation, much of it propelled by the discovery of mineral wealth and the impact of this discovery on the country's economic and social life. After the discovery of diamonds in

2

the 1860s on land incorporated into the Cape Colony and, in 1886, of rich gold deposits in the Transvaal region, parts of South Africa underwent an unprecedented process of speeded-up industrialization and modernization. The community dislocation and developing class conflicts that characterized industrialization in a country like Britain in the nineteenth century were echoed in compressed, distorted and often violent ways in South Africa, and were deeply intertwined with issues of race. It was this history which became increasingly important to Schreiner's life as a writer as she tried to intervene in and shape its course. *The Story of an African Farm* helped establish her as an important proponent of women's rights but her South African experience determined that feminism was increasingly fused with analysis and condemnation of other forms of social oppression, making Schreiner's a distinctive critical voice in the period.

Schreiner was educated at home by her mother, an education that was dominated by Wesleyan Christianity, and based on deep study of the Bible. Her first two novels, *Undine*[3] and *The Story of an African Farm*, detail the inner torment of children who question religious faith and suffer guilt and isolation as a result. In describing the anguished history of her own religious questioning, Schreiner described herself as becoming, at around the age of nine, a 'freethinker'. Freethinking, which denoted opposition to the organized Church and held that opinion should be based on reasoned knowledge, was associated by its opponents with Godless rationalism and materialism. This tumultuous intellectual and spiritual experience coincided with the break-up of Schreiner's family which followed her father's dismissal from the Wesleyan ministry for infringing rules on trading. The strains of providing for a large family had precipitated his misdemeanour, with the result that Gottlob and Rebecca could no longer care for their dependent children. Schreiner was initially sent to live with an older brother and sister, Theo and Ettie, at Cradock in the Karoo region of the Cape. These siblings were fiercely evangelical, and Schreiner experienced relentless persecution at their hands. There were, however, compensations even in this unsympathetic household as Schreiner was now living close to one of the best lending libraries in the colony. Over the next years, moving between differcnt relatives and family acquaintances, she began to read many of the important books that were shaping modern thought, including works by Charles Darwin, Herbert Spencer and John Stuart Mill.

In the Prelude to *From Man to Man*, the last of the three novels partly or wholly written while Schreiner was a young woman in South Africa, the five-year-old child, Rebekah, whispers a secret to her imaginary baby: 'I'm a person that makes stories! I write *books!'* (*FMM* 53). From early childhood there are records of Schreiner pacing up and down, 'clapping my hands', and telling herself a story she was creating out loud (*WSA* 382). She wrote journals, diary entries, small fragments of fiction and poetry and, by 1872, she was tackling larger-scale writing. By June 1873 she had begun *Undine*, her first novel, completed in February 1876. Around this time she also started to earn a living, working for the next six years as a governess on a series of Boer farms in the Cradock and Tarka districts of the Cape. In all accounts of Schreiner's life, including her own, despite being sometimes exhausted by overwork and personally unhappy, this was her most fertile and productive period as a writer. Dissatisfied with *Undine*, she went on to reuse some of its scenes in *The Story of an African Farm*. In the spring of 1881, with help from her family and money saved from governessing, Schreiner travelled to England, the place she called 'home'. Abandoning her original plan to undergo medical training because of ill health, Schreiner concentrated on finding a publisher for her novel and, after several rejections, *The Story of an African Farm* was accepted by Chapman & Hall on the advice of their reader, George Meredith, and appeared in two volumes in January 1883.

African Farm brought Schreiner many admirers including the historian W. E. Lecky, Sir Charles Dilke and Gladstone. More important, it acted as a ticket of entry into 1880s radical circles and the debates that were raging there. Schreiner met, befriended and corresponded with many of the key figures involved in socialist and feminist politics. The cultural and intellectual atmosphere in London was enormously lively and exciting, and Schreiner later ticked off her friend Edward Carpenter for failing to recognize the importance of such an environment for those denied the fellowship and stimulus of formal education: '*You have been over fed*. We are dying of hunger'

(*OSL* 147; Schreiner's emphasis). However, it was also a daunting place for a single young woman. Having decided that she would make her living by writing, Schreiner set about completing a second novel, *From Man to Man*. The asthma-related symptoms which had begun while she was still in South Africa, and affected her health for the rest of her life, often prevented her from working, and she frequently moved lodgings in London and between London and Sussex, Derbyshire, Bournemouth and Harrow in search of a place where she could breathe easily.

These physical difficulties are an eloquent, if distressing, aspect of Schreiner's life. The evidence suggests that she suffered from asthma-related respiratory problems and, later in her life, from problems with her heart. She also suffered from repeated bouts of measles and possibly from typhoid. She often wrote to friends about her condition and they occasionally suggested remedies or, like her close friend Havelock Ellis, prescribed treatments. Some critics and biographers have over-emphasized her illness, seeing it as evidence of Schreiner's neurotic temperament, while others have speculated about whether the drugs she took were in fact responsible for her symptoms (*OSB* 336).[4] Perhaps one way to think about Schreiner's illness – which avoids becoming entrammelled in unanswerable issues about diagnosis – is to understand it as one means by which Schreiner narrated herself to others, providing motive for actions which otherwise might have been unaccountable. Illness precipitated physical movement – from one lodging house to another, from one area of a country to another, or from one continent to another. Geographic movements in turn were bound up with relationships and with the brute financial issues which were an ever-present feature of Schreiner's life. She frequently worried about money, seeking advice about which publishers she might trust to deal fairly with an inexperienced author. In 1883, she wrote around a dozen times to Philip Kent, after he reviewed *African Farm* sympathetically, asking for advice about negotiating with publishers (Chapman, who brought out the book, offered her £10 for the copyright). As she became more famous, and *African Farm* was translated into other languages, it brought her more income but letters indicate an ever-present anxiety about the financial remuneration from her writing.[5] Her elder brother Fred helped to support her and, in turn, her illness was experienced as part of an ongoing struggle to reconcile the aspiration for independence with the significant material and emotional challenges facing single women.

Schreiner often needed breathing space in her writing too, but that also proved difficult. She worked on *From Man to Man* through 1884 and 1885, commenting on the process in letters to Havelock Ellis. Ellis, who would later become the country's leading sexologist, had fallen in love with Schreiner after reading *African Farm* and they became close friends and corresponded daily. Schreiner was hard at work on her novel, but often unhappy with the results: 'I have so cut up and changed the thing...that there is hardly anything left and I don't know how to put it together. This afternoon I nearly got up and burnt the whole MS.... I think it was the Devil made me unpick it' (*LOS* 28). Unpicking and condensing, however, was what she felt impelled to do. A few months later in November 1884 she wrote again to Ellis that her book 'grows smaller and smaller. I am sure that all I am doing is improvement. Condense, condense, condense' (*MOS* 224). In Virginia Woolf's *Orlando* (1928) a cloud appears at the beginning of the nineteenth century to steal damply over England, causing everything to become heavier and more muffled. Sentences swell and adjectives multiply in Woolf's parody of the aesthetic and moral weightiness and dullness of the Victorian period, emblematized in its solid ornamented architecture and its triple-decker novels. Woolf saw it as a world of misplaced faith in external realities which she sought to recast in a prose that was sharply attentive to inner experience. For Schreiner, too, the solidity and scale of Victorian literary realism increasingly seemed too unwieldy a style to capture the realities she sought to portray. 'I am working too. But my story gets smaller, and smaller, and smaller. I can't help myself. I'm driven on to make it smaller'. (*MOS* 249)

The heart of Schreiner's novel at this point concerned the position of women, and she later described it as 'the most womanly book that ever was written' (*MOS* 447). She began to believe that science, rather than fiction, might cut through the complexity of the topic and was inspired to 'attack these sex questions didactically' (*OSL* 115). She agreed to write an

6

introduction to a centennial reissue of Mary Wollstonecraft's *Vindication of the Rights of Woman* which she hoped would 'hold the substance of all my thoughts on the man and woman question' (*OSL* 136). But writing in 1888 to Havelock Ellis she confessed that this, too, was proving problematic, and that instead of scientific survey, she found herself writing allegories: 'I've tried to keep them out but I can't.... It's so easy for a mind like mine to produce long logical arguments, or strings of assertions, but when I have done it I feel such a "valch" [loathing] against it: that is only the material; it has to be combined and made alive.' (*OSL* 142)

Finding a form in which the 'material' of her arguments for social renovation could come alive was Schreiner's primary creative task through the rest of her life. Between 1887 and 1889, staying now mostly in Italy where she went to recover from a mental and physical collapse, Schreiner wrote short, lyrical pieces which she called 'dreams'. They are brief, compressed parables, intensely modern in theme yet allegorical, and redolent with the cadences and rhythms of Biblical prose. They focus on love and desire, equality and freedom, maternity, socialism and labour, and were published in two collections that appeared at the end of 1890 and in 1893 called, respectively, *Dreams* and *Dream Life and Real Life*. Some commentators and reviewers were disappointed that the long-awaited next work by Schreiner was not another novel, but were nevertheless moved by the 'ascetic unrestful hope' conveyed in Schreiner's prose.[6] Schreiner's allegories and short stories contributed to a widespread literary experimentation taking place at the fin de siècle: Oscar Wilde published one in *The Woman's World*, the magazine he edited between 1887 and 1889, and they were championed by the symbolist and 'decadent' poet and critic Arthur Symons.

By the time *Dreams* appeared, however, Schreiner had left Europe and returned to South Africa. Apart from brief trips to England she lived in the country of her birth for the next twenty years. A number of her siblings were already established as public figures there, her brother William in particular becoming a prominent Cape politician who served as Prime Minister towards the end of the 1890s. Schreiner found herself fascinated by South Africa, and began to write about its history and people. In 1894, she married a farmer called Samuel Cronwright, and the following year they had a child which sadly lived for only a few hours. However, she could not live on the farm her new husband worked – her asthma became too severe – and the couple moved to Kimberley, apparently with the view that Schreiner should complete *From Man to Man* and another work and make them financially independent (*LiOS* 271).

But the tumultuous political events of the 1890s, culminating in war between the British and the other major group of white colonizers, the Boers, in 1899, got in the way of this domestic planning. Increasingly these events seemed to call for urgent interventions and thus different kinds of writing. Although Schreiner used a novella-length allegoric story, *Trooper Peter Halket of Mashonaland*, to attack the actions of Cecil Rhodes' British South Africa Company, much of her writing from this point was non-fiction, as if the situation to be confronted could not risk too much literary transformation. She did, though, work again on *From Man to Man* in this period, incorporating more explicitly themes of race into its feminist narrative. In South Africa, class and gender were complicated by race and their attendant injustices were, Schreiner feared, peculiarly magnified and intensified as a result. In trying to make sense of the effects of modernization there, she became a fervent critic of the monopoly capitalism dominating the Cape economy and a determined opponent of Britain and empire. Towards the end of the first decade of the twentieth century, her voice became more prophetic, as her hope for South Africa's future stumbled, and her politics more local, supporting those disadvantaged by discriminatory laws. The last extended period of her life spent outside South Africa coincided with the First World War, when Schreiner lived alone in England, estranged from her husband, suffering badly from a heart condition and raging against the depravity and waste of war. Although unwell, she wrote various short pieces on conscientious objection and pacifism, as well as beginning a book about war, part of which was published after her death as 'The Dawn of Civilisation'.

Announcing her death in December 1920, the *Athenaeum* concluded that Schreiner 'was the woman of the single work' – *The Story of an African Farm*.[7] There were some, however, who did not agree with this assessment. *Woman and Labour*, dubbed by its publisher 'the Bible of the Woman's Movement', appeared in

1911, and was widely hailed and celebrated by suffragettes. Winifred Holtby, surveying 'Writers of South Africa' for *The Bookman* in 1929, praised the range of Schreiner's work and the 'prophetic clarity' of her insights into social change, while in 1955, celebrating the centenary of Schreiner's birth, the South African communist activist, and editor of the *African Communist*, Michael Harmel, regretted that Schreiner had been so often associated exclusively with feminist goals. Instead, he argued for Schreiner's wider political importance as a 'courageous champion of the oppressed, the weak, the exploited, wherever they might be'.[8] But the publication in 1924 of *The Life of Olive Schreiner* and an edition of *The Letters of Olive Schreiner* by her husband and literary executor, undoubtedly affected much future assessment. Cronwright presented Schreiner as a wayward genius, unfitted for sustained intellectual work, neurotic and mentally inflexible. One of Schreiner's recent biographers, the novelist and historian Karel Schoeman, acknowledges the zeal with which Cronwright carried out his duty to the wife he had lived apart from for many years (as well as the *Life* and *Letters*, Cronwright published Schreiner's first completed novel *Undine* (1929), her unfinished novel *From Man to Man* (1926), a collection of essays on South Africa, *Thoughts on South Africa* (1923) and a collection of short fiction, *Stories, Dreams and Allegories* (1923)). But Cronwright destroyed almost all the original material in his possession – letters, diaries and manuscripts – 'in an act of supreme literary vandalism'. Schoeman sharply concludes that his activities amounted to 'a largely successful if unconscious attempt to avenge himself posthumously on his wife' (*OALH* 35). The story of Schreiner's life and writing has now to be reconstructed from what remains. Certainly, though, many of Schreiner's friends disliked Cronwright (who was widely seen as arrogant, humourless and opinionated), and deliberately withheld letters in their possession, so a substantial body of correspondence has survived. In 2012, *Olive Schreiner Letters Online*, under the leadership of the sociologist Liz Stanley, has made freely available all Schreiner's extant letters currently lodged in archives in the United States, South Africa and elsewhere. Providing a far more accurate and extensive archive of Schreiner's correspondence, this is a scholarly venture that will hopefully precipitate major reassessment of Schreiner's life and work.[9]

9

From the early reviews of *African Farm* up until today, Schreiner has divided critics. During her own lifetime, her support for unpopular causes – siding with the Boers during the 1899-1902 conflict with Britain, or advocating conscientious objection during the First World War – made her enemies, and a critical orthodoxy emerged which emphasized her wasted talent. Her work and life began to be reassessed by feminist scholars in the 1970s and 1980s and, despite notoriously sharp treatment in Elaine Showalter's influential *A Literature of Their Own* (1978), Schreiner's importance as a writer and political actor has subsequently been widely recognized.[10] She has been hailed as a key figure of first-wave feminism and a unique voice articulating connections between sexuality, race and class. Her writing illuminates the intellectual, emotional and aesthetic processes attending Victorian secularization, and *The Story of an African Farm* has been read as the inaugurating 'New Woman' novel. Critics and writers including Doris Lessing, Dan Jacobson, J. M. Coetzee and Nadine Gordimer have attested to Schreiner's importance as a South African novelist, responsible for making the desolate Karoo landscape a topic of fiction for the first time, and clear-sighted in her starkly prescient warnings about the future of South Africa.[11]

This book begins with Schreiner's most popular work, *The Story of an African Farm*, setting this early novel in the context of Schreiner's evangelical upbringing and her effort to represent issues of faith, truth and social justice. It argues that Schreiner is able to combine the internal drama of religious doubt with the politics of feminism far more productively in *African Farm* than in her first completed novel, *Undine*. The second chapter focuses on Schreiner's feminism, examining her influential non-fictional tract, *Woman and Labour*, her short stories and allegories and her 'womanly' novel, *From Man to Man*. The final chapter turns to her distinctive contribution to political debate about gender, race and class in South Africa, which dominated much of her thinking and writing after returning to the country of her birth at the end of the 1880s. Throughout, it tries to convey something of Schreiner's energy and her humanity. In his biography, Cronwright did a good deal to attest to his wife's 'awful intensity', recalling guests at a select Cape Town dinner party becoming alarmed as, goaded and frustrated by Cecil John

Rhodes with whom she was arguing, she repeatedly banged her forehead with force against the table (*LiOS* 208). But Schreiner was also tender and funny and playful. Havelock Ellis recalls her trying to persuade him down a pathway during a stroll together, singing softly to herself, 'I have a donkey and he won't go'; or intoning seriously, as they viewed bronze vessels in the Louvre, 'A woman is...a ship with two holes in her bottom'.[12] She had an extensive network of friends, especially women friends. She frequently put people she knew in touch, sometimes helping young or financially struggling acquaintances with money.

Schreiner's imagination was recognizably forged in the evangelicalism of the nineteenth century but it was strange and original too. Writing about a destructive woman character in her novel *From Man to Man*, the narrative pauses momentarily as the woman goes, unbidden and for the first time in her life, into a man's bedroom and softly touches his clothes and brushes. It is a surprising and completely gripping scene, short, neutral in tone but thrilling and sensuous. It ends with the woman, Veronica, discovering an old-fashioned portrait case containing a daguerreotype photograph of a child, immediately recognizable to the woman as Bertie, the novel's beautiful young sister who Veronica will displace in the man's affection and attempt to obliterate, as she does the tiny picture: 'Quickly she put the case down upon the table, and, placing her large flat thumb on the face, she pressed; in a moment, the photograph had cracked into a hundred fine little splinters of glass' (*FMM* 130). The hands that gently touch the masculine objects in the room become chillingly destructive agents. In the same act, gendered oppression is complicated: women can act against women. Schreiner wrote to a friend: 'I don't know how it came into my head...It is in the place of a whole condensed chapter' (*OSL* 57). Schreiner is an important figure in the history of feminism and feminism's relationship to wider questions of social justice. She is also, as this short outline of her career shows, an original and challenging writer.

1

Evangelicalism, Freethought and Love: *Undine* and *The Story of an African Farm*

In December 1883, the journalist Henry Norman surveyed the state of contemporary fiction for the *Fortnightly Review*. '[O]ne place stood out' amidst the 'yachts, clubs, hansoms, and Piccadilly' which formed the backdrop of much formulaic novelistic fare. A 'weary flat plain of red sand' was the setting for a surprising recent novel, *The Story of an African Farm*, by an unknown author, Ralph Iron. Despite the 'very masculine name' on the title page, Norman was presciently convinced that he had been reading the work of a young woman. He warned his readers that the modest title would do little to prepare them for a novel which, with 'refreshing temerity', deals with the big issues of the day: faith, belief and knowledge, the position of women and the state of marriage, 'they all arise...over the horizon of this African farm'.[1]

Writing 70 years later, Schreiner's goddaughter, Olive Renier, recalls accounts by her mother and her friends of the impact in the 1880s of *The Story of an African Farm*.[2] As it quickly became known that 'Ralph Iron' was a young South African woman it seemed that 'Here was a genuine New Woman, who in the middle of her South African desert had somehow asked herself the same questions, about religion, about sex, that were being asked in and around the British Museum'.[3] Schreiner's most famous book appeared in two volumes in January 1883. It was the only one of her novels published in her lifetime and her only work constantly in print since. It tells of three children growing up on an ostrich farm in the Karoo region of the Cape Colony in the 1860s. Em is the English stepdaughter of the farm's owner, a Boer woman, Tant' Sannie; the beautiful Lyndall is Em's orphaned cousin; and Waldo is the son of the farm's benevolent and pious German overseer, Old Otto. Part I of the book focuses on Waldo's agonized loss of religious faith. His spiritual crisis is ironically accompanied by the arrival at the farm of Bonaparte Blenkins, adventurer and trickster, who inveigles his way into influence and power on the farm before finally being exposed and driven away. Wilful and ambitious, Lyndall leaves the farm for school, returning in Part II disdainful of girls' education but with a cogent feminist critique of the position of women. The young farmer, Gregory Rose, who in Lyndall's absence has become betrothed to Em, immediately becomes captivated by her. When Lyndall leaves secretly with the lover by whom she is already pregnant, Gregory seeks her out and disguises himself as a woman in order to nurse her to her death.

Amidst the turns of this more and less strange narrative, Waldo and Lyndall are the novel's questioners: both are attracted, but neither are saved, by the promise of modernity. Only the conformist Em lives on at the end of the novel, though with insight enough to understand that she pays a heavy price for conventionality. When, eventually, Gregory returns to her he is a husk of a man and Em poignantly reflects on the fragility of desire and hope as she recalls a childish ardent wish to play with a forbidden workbox, full of coloured reels of yarn. At long last given permission to take the box, she tells Waldo that she opened it only to find 'all the cottons were taken out' (*SAF* 266). She will be married, but to a man whose heart has followed Lyndall to the grave.

African Farm touched a chord 'in and around the British Museum' with its treatment of religion and sex. But if its themes were readily recognizable, they were also unsettled and unsettling, and readers were affected in new ways. The structure of disillusionment and moral readjustment so familiar in Victorian novels is reconfigured in the novel's odd combination of styles and genres, and through the strange intensity of its prose. The relatively conventional narrative of the first part of the book includes realism, Dickensian farce and naturalism. The second part, however, introduces an almost bewildering range of forms: they include first person plural spiritual autobiography,

Bunyanesque allegory, melodrama, epistolary narrative, feminist polemic and provincial satire. *African Farm* is a novel of ideas and the first 'New Woman' novel, a decade before the phrase was coined. Its giddying stylistic diversity is held together by the farm itself: apart from one chapter, everything takes place there. Figures from outside arrive and leave, ushering in change; characters depart but their stories are narrated only once back on the farm. Schreiner's novel is also the first of a new genre of South African farm novel (or *plaasroman*), and the colonial setting of the farm is central to its overall effect.

In the twentieth century, *African Farm* has been compared to Emily Brontë's *Wuthering Heights*. While this comparison highlights common themes of childhood experience and the symbolic resonance of the narrative's geographic setting, it also underlines the sense that *African Farm*, as much as *Wuthering Heights*, does not readily belong in the Victorian novel tradition. Like Brontë's text, *African Farm* owes more to Schreiner's reading of Romantic poetry – as well as her study of philosophy and social commentary. In the opening scene of the novel, the loose red sand, dry karoo bushes and unremitting heat of the African farm setting which dominates so much of the novel is initially transfigured by the effects of moonlight: 'The full African moon poured down its light', suffusing the lonely landscape with 'a weird and an almost oppressive beauty', picking out clumps of prickly-pears that 'lifted their thorny arms, and reflected, as from mirrors, the moonlight on their broad, fleshy leaves', and glinting on the zinc roof of the outbuildings 'with a quite peculiar brightness, till it seemed that every rib in the metal was of burnished silver' (*SAF* 1). The first human character identified in this glinting, near-magical world is the sleeping Tant' Sannie, fully-clothed in her bed, and dreaming of the sheep's trotters eaten at supper: 'She dreamed that one stuck fast in her throat, and she rolled her huge form from side to side, and snorted horribly' (*SAF* 2). The shift in register, from ethereal moon-drenched landscape to shockingly brute corporeality, is typical of the novel's unsettling effects.

KNOWING AND BEING TAKEN IN: WALDO, FAITH AND TRUTH

At the age of 12 Schreiner wished to be above all things clever and wise. *Undine*, her first attempt at a novel, opens with the child Undine addressing her pet monkey, Socrates, with a wistful 'I wish we knew' (*U.* 4). 'Knowing', for both Schreiner and her autobiographical protagonist, lies on the other side of an emotionally wrenching experience of lost Christian faith. For Undine (as for Schreiner herself) losing faith is a protracted and violent process of rejection and expulsion: it means recognizing and then refusing the hypocrisy, manipulation and bullying which characterizes the evangelicalism of her family and associates. Schreiner's home education was predominantly Wesleyan, and based on a deep and detailed study of the Bible. Evangelical Wesleyanism emphasized the pain and suffering, and the necessity for endurance, which man's sinfulness had brought upon him. Wesley wrote of humans 'bent to back-sliding, a natural tendency to evil' (quoted *WSA* 132). Such ideas appear prominently in Schreiner's early fiction as the 'hellish voice' of the 'true Bible Christian', which plagues her characters with the torments of lost faith (*SAF* 256–7). Like the young Jane Eyre before her, Undine learns early lessons about power: being bullied and powerless is terrible, but there are other things that are even worse. When Waldo, in *The Story of an African Farm*, eventually articulates his bitter life lesson – 'There is no God... *not anywhere*' – the narrator bluntly notes that there is no aid for him, not even from Lyndall who 'instinctively' draws back from him and accuses him of madness: 'In the day of their bitterest need all souls are alone' (*SAF* 69).

Nor does turning the tables on misused power bring any simple or immediate benefit. For Jane Eyre, at last silencing Mrs Reed with the force of her passionate denunciation, the elation of victory swiftly gives way to remorse represented by passion's 'black and blasted' remnants.[4] Similarly, when Undine gathers her courage and refuses to go to the chapel service her 'dried hide' grandfather insists that she attend, she makes him 'conquered for the first time in his life; conquered by a little child'. But, like Jane, Undine's victory undoes her: she goes into the garden and weeps, for 'Has not the victor's fate been, from

15

the beginning, to lie down and weep?' (*U.* 69). Questioning religious or social convention is tantamount to expulsion from a sense of home and belonging, and is accompanied by catastrophic loneliness. *The Story of an African Farm* opens with an image of misused power on a grand scale. Waldo, a small and terrified child, lies awake as his father sleeps in the outbuilding the pair occupy. Old Otto, the farm's German overseer, has ended the day reading aloud from Matthew 7 – '*For wide is the gate, and broad is the way, that leadeth to destruction*'. His son listens in the dark to the ticking of his father's hunting watch and, with each tick, hears the inexorable beat of another soul lost to eternal hell: '"Dying, dying, dying!" said the watch... Oh, the long, long ages of the past... Oh, God, the long, long eternity, which has no end! The child wept, and crept closer to the ground'. When William Paley published his influential *Natural Theology* in 1802, the intricacy of the watch's internal mechanism was presented as an analogy of divine purposiveness and design: as there is a watchmaker, so there is a God. But for Waldo, on lonely 'watch' during the night, feeling obscurely responsible yet impotent in the face of so much suffering, there is only horror in a Creator so pitiless about His children's suffering (*SAF* 3–4).

Waldo's sense that he is abandoned is confirmed when his fervent prayer that God show him a sign of His presence – by sending flames to engulf the boy's 'sacrifice' of a mutton chop, saved from that day's dinner – is unanswered. God's absence from the farm is also echoed and replayed in its other human inhabitants. This is a world bereft of good parents. Waldo's father, Otto, is the farm's most kindly adult, and his cabin is 'the one home the girls had known', filled with 'golden memories' (*SAF* 20). But he is gullible: faith makes him a dupe and, as a result, he too effectively abandons the children. When a stranger, Bonaparte Blenkins, arrives on the farm, Otto can only view him through a distorting haze of Biblical teaching: 'I was a stranger, and ye took me in', he reads, seeing not 'the bloated body nor the evil face of the man, but... the form that long years of dreaming had made very real to him' (*SAF* 23). Schreiner works the irony of being 'taken in', or deceived, using the Biblical phrase as her chapter heading, and underlining her theme in hard-headed Tant' Sannie's reaction to Bonaparte's appearance, ordering him off the farm, 'I'm not a child...You can't take *me* in!' (*SAF* 17).

In fact, Tant' Sannie is quickly manipulated by Bonaparte because she is ignorant and easily flattered. Otto is 'taken in' because his gullible faith precludes questioning. He is wrongly and guiltily childlike, leaving the real children exposed to Bonaparte's scheming. The comedy and irony which lighten the first part of the novel in the depiction of the scheming, winking Bonaparte, vanish when he beats Waldo, in a horrific parody of paternal authority: 'I shall act as a father to you, Waldo, I think we had better have your naked back' (*SAF* 92). There is nothing in Otto's goodness that is sufficiently redemptive to set alongside his failure to protect the children and, when Bonaparte demands that Waldo answer him 'as you would your father, in whose place I now stand', he speaks a warped truth (*SAF* 89). Both Bonaparte and Otto together signify that proper paternal authority is nowhere to be found: the children are literally and symbolically orphaned and their fatherlessness signals the absence of God on the farm. All through the 'dreadful night' which follows his beating, Waldo prays 'and he got no answer' – and this is the last prayer he makes in the novel (*SAF* 93).

Bonaparte is the first of a series of outsiders who bring disruption and change to the farm. A parody of his historical namesake, he gains power through the deceitfulness playfully encapsulated in his other name, Blenkins, which derives from 'blench', meaning to elude or cheat. He tricks his way into Tant' Sannie's favour and undermines Otto who is ordered off the farm. Otto succumbs to his weak heart and dies and Bonaparte's position seems unassailable until Tant' Sannie overhears him wooing her wealthy niece and drives him from the farm with a well-aimed shoulder of mutton from a barrel of salt meat. In *Undine*, Schreiner is explicitly contemptuous of the religious community in which she grew up. Undine refuses to attend the revivalist services because she sees the audience as dominated by bullying, over-fed and complacently cruel hypocrites (*U.* 57–60). The devout Mrs Snappercaps, in whose wagon Undine travels to the newly-discovered diamond mines in South Africa, is semi-literate, envious and venal. Toothless, a fat and dirty baby (named 'Master John Wesley') at her breast, her religion is a means to control those around her (*U*. 250–2). In *African Farm*, by contrast, the critique of religion is symbolized rather than directly represented: Bonaparte acts as a swaggering, parodic sign of its ethical inefficacy and hypocrisy. Religion's failure is foundational, and it extends to the idea of truth itself.

Storytelling is central to Bonaparte's deception, and the value of stories is regularly put in question in the novel. Losing belief in stories suggests the larger loss of faith in the stories of Christianity that Victorians suffered. The benign but failed father, Otto, predictably loves melodramatic romances: to him, 'a story was no story. Its events were as real . . . as the matters of his own life' (*SAF* 61). It is Lyndall who questions Bonaparte's stories, recognizing them as tall tales. Her challenge, 'And how do we know that the story is true, Uncle Otto?' reverberates through Victorian culture, as does Otto's agitated repost - 'If we begin to question everything – proof, proof, proof, what will we have to believe left?' (*SAF* 22). The text condemns his response in relation to Bonaparte, though Schreiner at the same time knows that Otto's desire for belief is a real and potent need. The penultimate chapter of the novel provocatively concludes that 'Without dreams and phantoms man cannot exist'. It is imperative, nevertheless, that modernity discover its own 'new-tinted' dream (*SAF* 260). Schreiner became clearer and clearer, as her life progressed, that this dream must include social justice – and this is a quality entirely absent from the African farm.

Waldo's first attempt to survive the bleak meaninglessness which threatens him as a consequence of his loss of faith is through creative making. He confesses to Em that he has a secret – '*I have made a machine*' (*SAF* 43; Schreiner's emphasis). Waldo's model sheep-shearing machine allows him to imagine a way out of the farm and into social prestige, modernity and power, as he dreams of it being used the world over. The pleasure he feels re-connects him to a restored and nurturing God: he feels 'a sense of a good, strong something folding him round' (*SAF* 64). Symbolically, this is God as protector-lover and progenitor: Waldo's sheep-shearing machine has taken nine months to make. When Bonaparte sees it, and praises it, Waldo cannot tell what is coming, for 'There was never a parent who heard deception in the voice that praised his child – his first-born' (*SAF* 73). When

Bonaparte crushes the machine underfoot the narrative turns not to Waldo's reaction but to his dog, Doss, who goes to play with a beetle:

> hard at work trying to roll home a great ball of dung it had been collecting all the morning; but Doss broke the ball, and ate the beetle's hind legs, and then bit off its head. And it was all play, and no one could tell what it had lived and worked for. A striving, and a striving, and an ending in nothing. (SAF 74)

The displacement from Waldo's fathomless grief to a dog at play – symbolically ushers out, in one destructive act, the Christian world. Doss can be seen to represent instead a Darwinian one, where humans are no more important than animals. All life is the product of the processes of adaptation, random variation and natural selection which Darwin's *Origin of Species* (1859) described. For some Victorians who found their faith in God shaken, this world seemed a chaotic place. It was capricious and wasteful, making life a chance occurrence and death a meaningless event. Modern science, to these minds, was responsible for this degraded, meaningless and materialist place. However, Waldo's despair – and Schreiner's – is about the arbitrariness of a 'great individual Will': if God is not to be trusted with a dung beetle, 'the least of these my brethren', what hope have suffering humans? (*FMM* 179; Matthew 25). For Schreiner, as for many other Victorians, science instead held the key to a route out of despair and into a more enlightened future.

By the 1880s there had been powerful and decisive developments in the place of science in Britain's intellectual life. In books, periodical essays, speeches, evidence to Royal Commissions, institutional alliances, professional practices and publishers' offices a newly influential group of (mainly) men were successfully establishing the authority of science. They included Darwin, Herbert Spencer, Thomas Henry Huxley, John Tyndall, Francis Galton and Karl Pearson. They were not a homogeneous group: indeed they were frequently in dispute with each other, but they were nevertheless shaping a modern, secular view of the world. Appealing to empirical evidence and committed to understanding the determinable laws of the universe, they sternly eschewed 'supernatural' explanation. As *African Farm* intimates, however, the journey from religious belief to secular science could be a long and difficult one, and more ambiguous than any simple opposition between religion and science allows.

Only after 'the footstep of Bonaparte Blenkins was heard no more at the old farm' does Waldo begin to recover and make sense of his world (*SAF* 100). The cultured European stranger who stops to rest at the farm, leaves him a book which, Schreiner explained to her friend Havelock Ellis, was meant to be Herbert Spencer's *First Principles* (1862). While the 15-year-old Schreiner was staying with relatives in an isolated part of Basutoland, a stranger ('like Waldo's Stranger exactly') knocked on the door requesting shelter from a night-time storm and lent the young girl a copy of Spencer's book: 'I always think that when Christianity burst on the dark Roman world it was what that book was to me. I was in such complete blank atheism. I did not believe in my own nature, or any right or wrong or certainty' (*OSL* 36). *First Principles* articulated the position that, in 1869, Thomas Huxley described by the neologism 'agnostic'. Spencer acknowledged an 'Unknowable' realm, but argued that science must necessarily be concerned with the phenomenal world, 'the Knowable', where test and verification were legitimate. Metaphysical notions, such as 'first causes', were not knowable and should thus be left well alone. But in the 'Knowable' realm, science brought (or could bring) law-like regularity to uncoordinated facts. In turn, the task of philosophy was to identify generalizations to which these laws conform. For Spencer, the overarching 'law' to which all of the knowable universe answers, from biological life to human ethics, is developmental or evolutionary. From germ-life to modern city, all forms move from simplicity to complexity, from homogeneity to heterogeneity, and from confusion to order. Spencer's 'synthetic philosophy', which emphasized evolutionary connectedness and implied direction, order and progress was, for many Victorians, an attractive lens through which to modify the capricious nature suggested in Darwin's Malthusian world of competition, chance and struggle for resources.[5]

Schreiner later said that she valued Spencer for helping her to believe in 'a unity underlying all nature' (*OSL* 37). In 'Times and Seasons', which opens the second part of *African Farm*, a first person plural voice recapitulates the processes of Waldo's spiritual crisis. This chapter, a compact spiritual autobiography, ends with the narrator's intense aesthetic pleasure and mental solace in finding pattern and regularity repeated throughout nature – in the blood-vessels of a drowned gander, the outline of a thorn-tree, the antlers of a horned beetle: 'Not a chance jumble.... all is part of a whole, whose beginning and end we know not' (*SAF* 118). This is a Romantic conception of natural harmony that Schreiner was able to synthesize with modern evolutionary biology. But the emotional transformations described and required are not easy. The 'Times and Seasons' narrator notes that: 'What a soul drinks in with its mother's milk will not leave it in a day...When a soul breaks free from the arms of a superstition, bits of the claws and talons break themselves off in him. It is not the work of a day to squeeze them out' (*SAF* 114). Rejecting Christian faith makes maternal nourishment mutate into a horrific bird-lover whose penetrations cause long-term damage. In Waldo's story, realism seems almost entirely inadequate to the task of representing the intellectual or emotional stages of this process. Instead, Schreiner shifts to allegory, a traditional and predominantly Christian form ironically brought to the farm by a cultured European who identifies himself as a sceptical unbelieving modern. The allegory he tells to Waldo is a parable about the methods of science: scientific truths mean arduous work, scaling the 'almighty mountains of Dry-facts and Realities', and accepting the tiny, partial contribution an individual can make to the slow accumulation of knowledge (*SAF* 123–33, 130). At the same time, in formally evoking Bunyan's *Pilgrim's Progress* the tale foregrounds Protestant and evangelical virtues of renunciation, suffering and martyrdom. 'Science' is accordingly transformed into a religious endeavour at the same time as the story rejects the consolations of religious belief. This is why Christians like Canon Malcolm McColl could conclude that *African Farm* showed its author to be a 'pure and pitying soul', while atheists, like Eleanor Marx's partner, Edward Aveling, understood the novel to perfectly demonstrate that 'Science has solved the problem of the hereafter'.[6] Content and form allowed each to be satisfied in different ways.

However, when Waldo eventually leaves the farm, armed with his small triumphs of enlightenment, it is to discover new kinds of isolation. The world outside the farm seems no better than inside, dominated as it is by cruelty, exploitation and an almost entire absence of sympathetic feeling between people. Outside is a place of unleavened poverty, exploitation and cruelty, where Waldo learns that 'You may work, and work, and work, till you are only a body, not a soul' (*SAF* 223). Religious or philosophical questions are here transformed into the currency of social inequality and injustice. Lyndall has also learned lessons about the wider world, though she mocks her former self when she returns to the farm from school, admitting that she has not fulfilled her 'old boast' to 'know everything that a human being can'. She has, however, learned something – though not from any finishing school which are aptly named, she tells Waldo, to 'finish everything but imbecility and weakness, and that they cultivate' (*SAF* 151-2). Where Waldo's subjective experiences, and the transformations they bring about, are signalled in formal disruptions (spiritual autobiography and allegory), we learn nothing directly about Lyndall's experiences. She returns to the farm with a fully formed critique of the position of women, forcing readers to ask how the novel makes connections between Waldo's agonized search for meaning and what Lyndall learns during her absence from the farm. This is another way of asking how the novel's 'twin concerns' – of religion and sex – are related.

LYNDALL AND LOVE

Shortly after avidly reading Spencer's *First Principles* in 1871 Schreiner moved to a small town, Dordrecht, to live with the family of a Wesleyan minister, Zadoc Robinson. Schreiner was 16, and living in a house that attracted young, educated people and was well-stocked with books by writers including Charles Darwin, Robert Chambers, Carl Vogt and John Stuart Mill. It was a period of great intellectual expansion for her. In *Undine*, which she began writing soon after leaving Dordrecht in 1872, Cousin Jonathan, the 'man with the mouth . . . forever hungering and seeking after something' initiates the child Undine into modern knowledge when they talk on the sea shore about the study of nature (*U.* 38, 53). He promises to send her books, pitying the orphaned girl but also desiring her: 'Cousin

Jonathan liked beautiful things – of the feminine gender' (*U.* 56). The narrative thus links Undine's intellectual awakening with sexuality and desire.

Cousin Jonathan's character was based, Schreiner explained, on Robinson. Schreiner's difficult relationship with the latter (who, she confirmed to Ellis, attempted to seduce her, as Cousin Jonathan does Undine) perhaps accounts for why there is such scant detail about the transformation from the questioning, suffering girl Undine, poring over her 'little brown Testament', to the resolutely freethinking and feminist young woman, with Mill's *Political Economy* lying next to her, that we encounter after a three years gap in the narrative (*U.* 64, 86). Mill's analysis links women's emancipation to liberal economics: like the labouring classes, women must also embrace the 'virtues of independence' in achieving justice and self-government.[7] There are hints that the books come from Cousin Jonathan but he is an object of repulsion and contempt for Undine and she sharply rejects his advances. There is no fortuitous coincidence between intellectual affinity and romantic love, or between love and independence, and the narrative is silent about Undine's intellectual formation.

When, some ten years later, Schreiner gave the manuscript of *Undine* to Havelock Ellis to read, she told him that she barely remembered it: 'I ought to have burnt it long ago, but the biographical element made me soft to it' (*LOS* 46). Ellis was fascinated by the glimpse it afforded into Schreiner's emotional and sexual past. As well as Robinson's advances, she also became involved in Dordrecht with a businessman called Julius Gau. Their engagement was announced to her family but then broken off. Schreiner was very distressed and some commentators speculate that she may have been (or suspected herself to be) pregnant. Years later, she was near panic-stricken to recognize people from this period of her life in a hotel in Italy, telling Ellis that they 'sit & jeer at me' (*MOS* 449).[8] It is easy to overlook how vulnerable Schreiner felt in the years following the breakup of her family home. Although her sexual history, and her anguished sense of being harshly judged, will necessarily remain topics on which critics can only speculate, there is substantial evidence of how her commitment to freethought isolated her amidst the predominantly Christian community she inhabited (*OSB* 78-9). The historian Laura Schwartz has shown how freethinking in this period was habitually associated in women with sexual permissiveness and unrespectability. Earlier century freethinking had often been accompanied by proposals to reorganize heterosexual relations. Connotations of 'free love' continued across the century, making women vulnerable to the charge that challenging religious belief necessarily implied sexual laxity and support for 'free unions'.[9]

In *Undine*, the feisty, questioning girl who grows up on a Boer farm embraces freethought and feminism. But when it comes to sexual attraction and love, it is as if too much anxiety attaches to her iconoclasm. Undine's love plot is terrible: it is stereotype and melodrama. The object of her attraction is an arrogant cold man, with 'disagreeable eyes', who passes 'commonplace conventional remarks', and expects Undine to conform to the dullest version of feminine propriety (*U.* 106). Meeting him by chance and seeing him look askance at the book she has been reading (by implication a volume by John Stuart Mill), she returns home and pulls out its pages, burning them one by one: 'I must be going mad...What makes me do this, and take such pleasure in doing it?', she asks – a question to which the text offers no convincing answer (*U.* 129). When her lover breaks off their engagement she decides to serve him by marrying his repulsive but wealthy father, George, with a view to thwarting the latter's plan to disinherit his son. The son, however, secures his own economic position by marrying into money and there is nothing for Undine to do but wait out a marriage into which she has sold herself. She gives birth to a baby who dies and, after the eventual death of her husband, she departs, abandoning the latter's fortune, for South Africa. There, poverty drives her to the newly discovered Diamond Fields where she finds work ironing. She eventually discovers that the man she loved is at the Fields but only sees him after his death, secretly spending the night before his burial with the body, from where she goes out alone under the stars and dies. By any reckoning, feminist or otherwise, this amounts to an uncomfortable plot.

Schreiner decided almost immediately not to publish *Undine* but instead reused some of its elements in *The Story of an African Farm*. She made, however, a crucial structural change by dividing up the two main themes – freethinking, associated with the loss of faith and intellectual awakening, on the one hand; and love, sex and the position of women, on the other. Instead of one female character, *African Farm* has one male and one female, Waldo and Lyndall. Lyndall's questioning and doubting 'If' (her response to Bonaparte's stories) implicitly aligns her with the questioning (proto-freethinking) Devil, with 'copper-coloured face, head a little on one side', who torments the would-be virtuous Christian child in the 'Times and Seasons' section (*SAF* 105). Nevertheless, in narrative terms she is safely distanced from the crisis of faith and freethinking which belong to Waldo (she is shocked by his declaration that there is 'no God' (*SAF* 69)). The accumulated associations between freethought and sexual impropriety are thus defused, and Lyndall's sexuality and her pregnancy can be represented on their own terms.

The child Undine rejects the punitive determinism associated with Calvinism, only to have a type of determinism re-emerge with a vengeance in her love life. Lyndall, by contrast, co-opts the narrative space left silent in *Undine* in order to analyse and critique determinism, and is able to put her John Stuart Mill to work (rather than pull out its pages and burn them). In a series of compelling images she pinpoints both biological essentialism and social oppression, brilliantly articulating the feminist themes that dominated debate about the position of women for the next two decades: economic dependency and marriage-as-prostitution, the hypocrisy of chivalry, the importance of maternity, and the relation between intellectual and sexual passion. The real harm, Lyndall knows, is the subjective component of social oppression whereby stereotype is internalized and feels inevitable: socialization fits women to their sphere as the Chinese woman's shoe fits her foot, 'exactly, as though God had made both – and yet He knows nothing of either' (*SAF* 155). She tells Waldo that: 'It is not what is done to us, but what is made of us... that wrongs us' (*SAF* 154).

Readers and critics of the novel have often shared Waldo's response to Lyndall. Awed by an eloquence sharply at odds with his own slow and hesitant speech, Waldo believes Lyndall must be capable of arguing into reality 'that new time' when 'to be born a woman will not be to be born branded' (*SAF* 162, 154). In an important sense, this is what happened as *African Farm*

25

helped to shape the debates that directed the transformation in women's social and legal position. Schreiner's friend, Mary Brown, records a Lancashire working woman recalling reading the parts about Lyndall over and over: 'I think there is hundreds of women what feel like that but can't speak it, but *she* could speak what we feel' (quoted *OSB* 121). A decade after *African Farm* appeared, the journalist W. T. Stead deemed Lyndall the original prototype for all the New Woman fiction of the 1890s, and Schreiner the 'the founder and high priestess of the school'.[10]

But there is also a hampering gap between a conceived ideal and its social and political enactment, one which Lyndall recognizes and identifies. In part this is what troubles readers trying to make sense of her enigmatic and elliptical statements about selfhood and love, and how these relate to her passionate feminism. In *Undine*, the unspoken link between freethinking and (unrespectable) sexuality can only be neutralized by associating the latter with suffering, will-lessness and determinism. It is as if Schreiner is bent on getting the punishment in first, before it can come from elsewhere. Lyndall, by contrast, is freed from the burden of carrying the narrative of lost faith and its accompanying fear and guilt and, as a result, has a very different relation to social and political activity. From a small child, we associate her with will, agency and autonomy. From her answer to Em's admiring enquiry as to how it is her beads never fall off her needle – 'I try', she answers, 'That is why' (*SAF* 5) – to her ability, in crisis, to silence Tant' Sannie and Bonaparte by the sheer exertion of her will, Lyndall confirms that the individual can exert influence on their world. The man she most admires is Napoleon Bonaparte, who 'had what he said he would have' (*SAF* 13–14). Comforting Waldo after his beating, she explicitly imagines a future in which, grown up, 'we shall have the power too' (*SAF* 94).

But this turns out to be no more the case for Lyndall than for Waldo. Having left the farm with her lover, by whom she is pregnant, we learn that she has banished him, and is dying in a hotel in a small town in the Orange Free State, following the birth (and death) of her child. Towards the end of her life, she makes a final effort to exert her will to live, insisting that 'Everything is possible if one is resolved' – but of course it is not, and Lyndall's eyes after this shine only with despair (*SAF* 250–1). Schreiner later vehemently argued that Lyndall's death was not a moral message about sexual impropriety but rather showed 'the struggle of helpless physical nature against the great forces of the universe – a sheer physical struggle' (*LiOS* 189).

But even if the reader accepts this, there is still the task of understanding what seems like a flip-side to the wilful and self-determining Lyndall that is associated with neediness and dependency. This flip-side includes the habitual focus on her physical tininess, and the eroticization of male dominance and female submission implied in her answer to her lover's query about why she loves him: 'Because you are strong. You are the first man I ever was afraid of' (*SAF* 206). Does Lyndall, in other words, seek to *be* Napoleon Bonaparte, or to be loved (and dominated) *by* him? John Kucich has made a powerful interpretation of these troubling aspects of Lyndall's character-ization in his exploration of masochism in fictional representa-tions of imperial and class politics. Though Schreiner's work and life have been discussed many times in relation to masochism, Kucich's analysis clarifies how evangelicalism helped to shape and propel masochistic fantasy. The fear and guilt that haunt Schreiner's children, he rightly notes, make up one side of evangelical rhetoric which emphasized God's punitive severity; the other side is 'certainty about salvation' which is associated with feelings of omnipotence.[11] In *African Farm*, Lyndall's self-exaltation and fantasies of control are manifestations of this other side of the evangelical message. Omnipotence in Kucich's psychoanalytic framework is a quality of the infant child's fantasy of a perfectly nurturing world amenable to its wishes and magically controlled by it. The sexualized dominance-and-submission analysed by Lyndall – 'you love me because you... want to master me' – and masochistically desired by her – she loves him because he is 'the first man I ever was afraid of' – is mixed with her wish for an 'omnipotent caretaker' (*SAF* 205, 206).[12] Her lover is transformed into a parent who must care for her – she looks at him 'as a little child might whom a long day's play had saddened' (*SAF* 207) – in an oscillation between fantasized omnipotence and infantile neediness. Another way of thinking about this is that Lyndall's plight, just as Waldo's, is about how autonomy and individuality sever the self from tradition and community. The latter is degraded and must be rejected but this in turn means that there is nowhere to belong – and suffering is the consequence.

Lyndall is accurate and devastating in her analysis of how tradition traps and confines women, comparing how she and Waldo 'both poor, both young, both friendless', with little to choose between them, would in fact be treated in entirely different ways in trying 'to make our way in life' (SAF 156). But the burdens of autonomy are also particularly heavy for women, as the young Schreiner well knew. In a particularly unhappy state of mind when she was working as a governess in South Africa, Schreiner discovered Ralph Waldo Emerson's Essays, later telling Havelock Ellis that 'Self-Reliance' helped her to recover from suicidal feelings (OSL 40). But Emerson's injunction to 'Trust thyself' and eschew both social convention and bogus consistency is illustrated only by the 'great men' his essay applauds.[13] Social forces are powerfully arrayed against the would-be self-reliant woman (SAF 183). Self-reliance risks, for Lyndall, a painfully solipsistic isolation from which she seeks escape, telling Waldo that she is 'swathed, shut up in self' (SAF 162). The text replays fairy-tale images of women frozen or asleep, awaiting their prince, as Lyndall weeps over Otto's grave for herself being 'alone, so hard, so cold', and imagines finding 'something nobler, stronger than I' to worship which might save her (SAF 209, 247).

But in reality, as Lyndall knows, romantic love is difficult and potentially a trap for women. The father of her baby 'was not my prince' and, facing the levelling experience of death, fairy-tale love cannot save her (SAF 246). Nor can her determination to have 'no conscience' in emulation of Napoleon Bonaparte (who Emerson described as an instance of 'the powers of intellect without conscience'[14]) in the end work either. It affords no comfort or hope for the future (SAF 176, 202). Intellect and will may be important components of independence but alone they cannot be women's sufficient goal. Instead, Lyndall envisages an 'infinite compassion for others' and the knowledge that 'happiness is a great love and much serving' (SAF 246, 249). This is an ethic fuelled by a religious culture which Schreiner – in common with other feminists, socialists and progressives in

28

this period – redirected for political purposes. She eventually became able again to use the 'older phraseology' to express this conviction that the universe is interconnected, and world, humans and God are not distinct. Her evangelical upbringing produced masochistic reverberations but it also fed an ethics of unity, encapsulated in the phrase: '*There is NOTHING but God*' (Schreiner's emphasis; *OSL* 213). Nevertheless, while social inequality and injustice remained rife in the present moment, service to others was inevitably potentially punitive for women: Undine spends much of her life enacting it, her selfhood (and life) draining away as she does. In *African Farm*, by contrast, it is an ethic spoken by Lyndall (and recognized as indispensible by her) but it is *enacted* by a man, dressed in women's clothes.

Gregory Rose is the callow young English farmer who initially courts Em. While Bonaparte Blenkins is the novel's colonial trickster and adventurer, Gregory parodies another type of colonial manhood. He casts himself as a suffering romantic hero, writing to his sister on the crested notepaper with which the family of 'an honest English farmer' reinvent themselves as nobility in the colony (*SAF* 140). Though engaged to marry Em, he is instantly infatuated when the beautiful Lyndall returns to the farm. Agreeing to Lyndall's proposition that he provide her with a semblance of respectability by marrying on her terms (he provides a name, but must expect no conjugal or other rights in return), Gregory subsequently tracks her down after she leaves with her lover, dresses himself in women's clothing, and lovingly nurses her to her death. He is described by the doctor as 'the most experienced nurse I ever came in contact with' (*SAF* 241).

Gregory's masculinity is lampooned by Lyndall and by Schreiner.[15] When Lyndall first meets him, she calls him a 'man-woman', one 'born for the sphere that some women have to fill without being born for it' (*SAF* 164). On departing the farm she leaves all the money she owns, £50, for Em, unsentimentally ironic about the value of Gregory's love which can so swiftly be transferred: 'Fifty pounds for a lover! A noble reward!' (*SAF* 209). But in doing so, she unwittingly honours a bet for the same amount, which she previously pledged to 'the first man who tells me he would like to be a woman' (*SAF* 153). Gregory's risible, parodied male masochism – Lyndall tells him that he is like 'a little tin duck floating on a dish of water, that comes after a piece of bread stuck on a needle, and the more the needle pricks it the more it comes on' (*SAF* 198) – is transmuted in his 'womanhood' into a model of other-oriented and serving love which retrieves him from ridicule. His role unsettles a predictable gendered script for the Victorian 'fallen' woman. As we have seen, Lyndall's determination to exert her will upon the world and act with 'no conscience' cannot ultimately prevail against either social forces or her own ethical intuitions. But Schreiner implies that if a new ethic of love is to be imagined and forged then men too need to join in. Lyndall, described by Elaine Showalter as the novel's 'first wholly serious feminist heroine', dies – but she does so with a final reference to the self-reliance Schreiner expresses whenever Lyndall looks into a mirror.[16] Her reflected eyes, saying 'We are not afraid ... we are together ... we will fight', indicate that while self-reliance is not sufficient it is yet a necessary starting-place for women (*SAF* 252).

ON THE FARM: WALDO AND COLONIALISM

In *Undine*, Schreiner transports her autobiographical protagonist to England. Known only through books and from her mother's memories, England was nevertheless preferable to a South Africa that seemed simply unthinkable as the setting of Undine's intellectual and sexual journey. The protagonists of *African Farm*, by contrast, fight things out at home. Like Schreiner herself, Waldo and Lyndall are at odds with their environment. When she returns to the farm after being at school Lyndall complains: 'There is not room to breathe here; one suffocates' (*SAF* 149). But in the world of the novel, the European 'outside' is no less problematic than the farm itself. Its symbols are often fragile: books are burned, inventions smashed underfoot and its representatives prove unreachable. When Waldo eventually sees his Stranger again, in the Grahamstown Botanic Gardens, class and poverty are barriers to their communication and he feels ashamed of himself for the first time, 'a low, horrible thing ... dressed in tancord' (*SAF* 228). When Lyndall agrees to go away with her lover rather than marry Gregory, she explicitly rules out any literal or symbolic move towards Europe: 'I will not go down country', she says, meaning English-speaking Cape Town, 'I will not go to Europe. You must take me to the Transvaal' (*SAF* 206). Lyndall follows the route taken by Dutch and Huguenot colonial settlers in the 1830s and 1840s. Known as the 'Great Trek', this eastward and north-eastward migration away from British control in the Cape Colony became a central element of Afrikaner nationalist mythology. Schreiner would later discuss it in detail in the essays she wrote on Boer life in the 1890s, but in *African Farm* it signals the bleak impoverished quality of the colonial world.

That world, inside and outside the farm, is inhospitable, offering its white inhabitants little succour. When Waldo 'goes out to taste life', he discovers a brutalized and dispossessed land, emblematized by the ox beaten to death by the master of the transport wagon which turns to him its 'great starting eyes' (*SAF* 226). Dreamy Waldo is a reader and interpreter of the signs of the culture's history and violence. While the child Lyndall revels in accounts of Napoleon Bonaparte's imperial ambition, Waldo sees a closer-to-home history in the 'Bushman' paintings which decorate the surface of the rocks. His imaginative identification with the 'Bushman' (or San) painters discovers their beauty despite a colonial culture which cannot acknowledge its own destructive violence: 'Now the Boers have shot them all' (*SAF* 16), Waldo notes.

Despite the symbolic and moral power conveyed in Schreiner's farm landscape, it is also a determinedly historical colonial place. What seems on first sight a static and unchanging pastoral world is in fact a dynamic, swiftly transforming colonial economy, indicated by the story's careful location in time. Bonaparte arrives in the summer of 1862, a drought year in the colony, but also a moment of significant transition. Ostrich farming, part of the Cape's economy throughout the century, underwent swift expansion between 1869 and 1874 as a result of both growing European demand and new entrepreneurial practices brought by British settlers.[17] Even more significant was the discovery of a diamond on the banks of the Orange River. When Em corrects the child Lyndall's dream of wearing diamonds in her hair, asking 'Where will you find them... The stones are only crystals that we picked up yesterday', Schreiner knows what the children as yet do not – that the chance find of a stone in 1867 marked the beginnings of South Africa's transformation into an industrialized mineral-exporting economy. By the time she wrote her novel Schreiner had lived at the Diamond Fields in Kimberley alongside thousands of migrant labourers trying to make a fortune and, in consequence, degrading the country's traditional tribal life.

In his review of *African Farm* for the socialist magazine, *Progress*, Edward Aveling insists that its 'local colouring' is incidental, and that with only 'slight modification' its setting could be 'an Indian bungalow or an English homestead', for it is primarily 'cosmopolitan and human'.[18] In fact, the link Schreiner makes between religious doubt, the pursuit of truth and the realities of social injustice depend upon the distinctive colonial world of the novel. What looks at first sight a static, rural culture, dominated by tradition, is in fact in the throes of disintegration under the new forces of industrialization and modernization. Towards the end of the book, Tant' Sannie, married for a third time to a husband with 'two farms, twelve thousand sheep', visits Em (*SAF* 167). Now so heavy she can barely move, she affectionately rails against Em's soap pot, which uses soda instead of traditional plants, foreseeing 'the itch, or some other disease' from such new-fangled inventions. She also tells Em, with great indignation, of having lately seen Bonaparte, now pretending to be a 'rich Englishman' and married to an elderly, ill and very wealthy Tant'. It is Tant' Sannie, and the tradition she represents, who is outwitted in the end. A winking Dickensian he may be, but Bonaparte nevertheless is the type of European adventurer whom Schreiner saw as destructive. With no roots in the land, their exploitative actions and wealth-grabbing are an integral part of imperial and colonial expansion.

Schreiner's would-be moderns, by contrast, suggest a more ambivalent relationship between place and belonging, tradition and modernity. The book ends with a rare moment of contentment for Waldo as he revels in the beauty of the late afternoon sun: 'shimmery afternoons' make life worth living, and as he sits in the yellow sunshine that tints 'even the air with the colour of ripe corn', he is happy (*SAF* 267–8). Waldo slips out of life at the end of the novel because, Schreiner implies, there is nothing sufficient to keep him in it. Nevertheless, there is still a tremulous note of hope. It is explicitly offered in the closing celebration of what Schreiner called 'universal unity': the sense of an unending evolutionary cycle which makes the tiny chickens that clamber over Waldo's body equal 'sparks of brother life' and takes the sting from death. More emotionally persuasive than Schreiner's intellectual reworking of evolutionary ideas, perhaps, is the aesthetic consolation that the warm beauty of the afternoon suggests, and the lingering sense that, after repose, 'the fierce agonizing flood of love for the living... will spring again' (SAF 268). This fittingly describes Schreiner's own unceasing struggle to keep hoping and working for a better future, as the next two chapters describe.

2

Sex Work: *Woman and Labour,* Stories and Allegories, *From Man to Man*

'England at last!' Schreiner wrote in her journal when she arrived there at the end of March 1881 (*LiOS* 145). She was to spend the next eight years in England and on the Continent, and this chapter focuses on how Schreiner participated in, and was influenced by, the distinctive political, scientific and aesthetic enthusiasms of the decade. Abandoning her initial plan to pursue medical training because of asthma-related health problems, Schreiner decided that 'scribbling will be my only work in life' (*LiOS* 151). As the recently published *African Farm* became 'a node of mutual recognition among young radicals in London', Schreiner had ready access to debates about social change that were gathering momentum in the first half of the decade.[1] One enthralled reader of the novel was the young Havelock Ellis, who later became Britain's foremost sexologist. He wrote to Schreiner, and they began a love affair that turned into a life-long friendship. With Ellis, Schreiner attended the newly-formed Progressive Association, a group of freethinkers and ethical socialists, and the Fellowship of the New Life.[2] The latter, dedicated to 'the cultivation of a perfect character in each and all', formed the nucleus of what was to become the Fabian Society. Here, Schreiner met Edward Carpenter, the utopian socialist, who became another close friend. She also befriended like-minded women: some, like her, were making reputations as writers, and most were involved in socialist or other progressive organizations. They included Eleanor Marx, Karl Marx's daughter, the poets Amy Levy and Dollie Radford, the children's novelist, Edith Nesbit, Alice Corthorn, who qualified as a doctor, and Margaret Harkness, a socialist activist and social-realist novelist.

At meetings of the Fellowship of the New Life, the topic of women's equality was soon known as 'Olive's subject' (*OSB* 145). The Victorian 'Woman Question' became more urgent in the atmosphere of the 1880s: agendas that had been formulated earlier in the century by Owenites and Chartists were seized upon and reinvigorated. As the population of Britain expanded over the second half of the century employment prospects and conditions for both middle- and working-class women were the focus of contention. Overt conflicts developed with organized male labour, but there were also strong alliances between socialists and feminists. Events such as the successful 1888 'matchgirls' strike at the Bryant and May match factory helped women gain confidence and skill in political activism. They aimed to organize in the same way as men to improve employment conditions, culminating in the formation of a Women's Trade Union Association in 1889, the Women's Industrial Council in 1894 and the National Union of Women Workers in 1895.

Universities had begun to open their doors to women: institutions in major northern cities, such as Leeds, admitted women on the same basis as men from its inception in 1874, while the University of London removed disabilities for women by 1877. In relation to family and marriage a series of legislative acts relating to married women's property, child-custody and divorce modified the unquestioned authority of husband and father within homes. Intellectual debate was correspondingly lively. Sexual difference was discussed in sharply opposing ways: on the one hand, evolutionary and other quasi-scientific theories were held by some definitively to prove women's biologically-rooted inferiority to men, their lesser capacity for reason and the use of intellect, or for sustained work and effort. Opposing such arguments, but often drawing upon and utilizing the same biological and evolutionary discourse, was a powerful assertion of women's moral superiority. The latter was held to be a sign of their more 'evolved' nature which was urgently needed to regenerate the public sphere.[3] Biological and evolutionary ideas about heredity were also central to the growing significance of the idea of eugenics. The prospect of explicitly controlling the quality of the population appealed to many emancipatory-minded women, as it made rational choice in marriage a key element of national health and progress.[4]

Indeed, in these years, a wide range of positions which have subsequently loosely been labelled 'feminist' existed: they include the idea of moral reform promoted by social purity campaigners, 'equal-rights' feminists influenced by John Stuart Mill's liberal individualism and socialist feminists with a keen eye on class and social hierarchy. At times these groupings came together in response to issues that served to radicalize women. One example is the opposition to the Contagious Diseases legislation which, from the 1860s, allowed authorities to arrest and medically examine suspected prostitutes in port towns, thereby enshrining in law double standards of sexual behaviour for men and women. This discriminatory legislation was repealed in the 1880s, by which time many women involved in campaigning against it had learned to be formidable organizers and public speakers. Protests erupted too after the publication in 1885 of the journalist W. T. Stead's sensational revelations in the *Pall Mall Gazette* about the seduction and procurement for prostitution of young girls, in a series of articles entitled 'The Maiden Tribute of Modern Babylon'.[5] These highly visible issues provided models for organization and action which extended into other areas of public life thought of as needing 'purification'. They were also influential for alternative types of political activism, including the budding suffrage movement.

Alongside the campaigns and practical initiatives which increasingly characterized the socialist and women's movements was a strong commitment to the transformative energies of art. William Morris was working to develop a socialist aesthetic based on the values of non-alienated work.[6] Edward Carpenter's long, Whitmanesque prose-poem, *Towards Democracy*, appeared in 1883 and sounded, according to Eleanor Marx's partner, Edward Aveling, 'the first inarticulate notes of the sighing of the people for the land'.[7] Experiments in new ways of living – including communes, vegetarianism and dress reform – were accompanied by aesthetic experimentation which began to reshape traditional Victorian literary forms, a process aided by changes in the literary marketplace. By the early 1890s the once ubiquitous three-volume novel (the 'triple-decker') had almost vanished. The powerful lending library system which had dominated mid-Victorian publishing was diminishing in importance while booming magazine and periodical titles favoured shorter writing. The term 'short story' began to be heard in the 1880s, and the form was used to great effect in the following decade by 'New Women' writers whose fiction explored new female aspirations and identities.

African Farm contributed to this coupling of literary experimentation and political change. Quickly acknowledged as an innovative and politically radical new voice, Schreiner set about revising *From Man to Man*. She had begun (and possibly completed a version of) this novel in South Africa and she worked on it between 1884 and 1886, and again in 1888 when she wrote 'The Child's Day', a prelude to the main story. But by the mid-1880s she was also often deflected from novel-writing by reading, thinking, talking and note-taking about gender issues ranging from modesty to monogamy, and from the effects of celibacy to the persistence of sexual desire during pregnancy and lactation. She had begun to want to write 'a purely scientific collection of facts' about sexuality and the position of women (*LOS* 141). Both of these projects – novel and 'scientific' tract – proved problematic, however. Although she periodically returned to *From Man to Man* it was still unfinished at her death and she never again wrote a novel. Her plans to write on 'sex evolution' were also delayed although they did eventually bear fruit, as *Woman and Labour*, which appeared in 1911 when it was trumpeted as 'the Bible of the Woman's Movement'. An influential text for the suffragettes and early twentieth-century feminism more generally, *Woman and Labour* is judged by the sociologist Liz Stanley to be 'the most important analytic work to emerge from feminism over the period of Schreiner's life, and indeed for a good while after her death'.[8]

In its introduction, Schreiner explains that the 1911 text was originally part of a much longer work, mostly written in the 1880s, which was destroyed when British soldiers looted her Johannesburg home during the Anglo-Boer war of 1899–1902. After her death this claim was contradicted by her husband, Cronwright, who believed that she was temperamentally incapable of writing a synthesizing survey on such a scale (*LiOS* 353–7).[9] Though there is no definitive evidence, Schreiner certainly had in mind in the 1880s the type of wide-ranging work she describes at the beginning of *Woman and Labour*. She sketched a plan for such a book to a friend in 1886, and also wrote to potential publishers about a series of essays on 'Sex Growth' (by which she meant an evolutionary account of sexuality and gender) which she intended would form the basis of a book-length work (*OSL* 103–4, 141). Her ambition to write a major work on women's position and sexuality is clear.

But it is equally clear that problems of form kept intruding. Schreiner admitted to Ellis that while trying to shape analytic arguments about 'sex evolution', she could not stop writing allegories, and in the introduction to *Woman and Labour* she explains that she found it impossible to convey the emotion attached to abstract thoughts in any form other than allegory or what she called 'dreams' (*OSL* 142; *WL* 16). The 'material' of feminist argumentation needed an aesthetic ideal to be made 'alive' (*OSL* 142). Allegory allowed Schreiner to manage the contradictions with which she grappled, between individual and typical experience, between self-realization and self-sacrifice, and between materialism and idealism. She turned allegory to the service of political critique, while using its formal qualities of compression and lyricism to infuse ideas developed in her scientific reading with spiritual intensity. Aesthetic transformation was crucial to producing and conveying hope which Schreiner knew was an indispensable element in aspiring for social justice.

All of the works discussed in this chapter – the feminist tract *Woman and Labour*, the unfinished novel *From Man to Man*, and many of the allegories and short stories collected as *Dreams* (1890), *Dream Life and Real Life* (1893) and *Stories, Dreams and Allegories* (1923) – draw strongly on Schreiner's experiences in the 1880s and the decade's hopeful political atmosphere. There are common themes: evolutionary theory and social Darwinism, sexual desire and its renunciation, masculinity and paternity, and ideas of production and reproduction. Prostitution is central to the two longer texts, *Woman and Labour* and *From Man to Man*. Schreiner studied prostitution intensively in the mid-decade, reading and discussing published sources, and meeting and talking to prostitutes. In 1907 she told her husband Cronwright: 'You will see that if you read my novel [*From Man to Man*] all other matters seem to me small compared to matters of sex, and prostitution is its most agonising central point' (*LOS* 265). But the long years of writing both *Woman and Labour* and *From Man to Man* also show how 'matters of sex' became increasingly complicated for Schreiner after her return to South Africa in 1889. Imagining a better future for women was more complex within the inequities of colonial culture and Schreiner had to find alternative and modified visions of modernity and progress from those which dominated both socialist and feminist metropolitan debate in the 1880s. In the process, she increasingly saw feminist aspirations as legitimate only when they were connected up with other, and wider, claims for social justice.

PRODUCING THE FUTURE: *WOMAN AND LABOUR*

When *Woman and Labour* appeared in 1911 it captured much of the energy and hope of the earlier 1880s, but it also illustrated how problematic ideas about evolution and progress could prove to be within feminist debates. The book was greeted by the suffragette Emmeline Pethick-Lawrence as a 'scripture infinitely precious' for the cause of women's emancipation.[10] It makes simple demands for women's access to work, for their right to the employment and income-earning opportunities available to men and the education and training appropriate to such work. These demands were encapsulated in the book's opening and repeated refrain: '*Give us labour and the training which fits for labour!*' (*WL* 33; Schreiner's emphasis). It argues that there is an historical and evolutionary inevitability about the liberation of women into a full role in economy and society, and the removal of their legal, social and economic disablements. Writing over twenty years later, Vera Brittain confessed that she still 'tingle[d] with excitement' at the memory of its confident insistence that women '*take all labour for our province!*'.[11]

Schreiner immediately modifies this claim for equality of opportunity, however: '*We demand this, not for ourselves alone, but for the race*' (*WL* 33). Schreiner is not simply extending to women

John Stuart Mill's liberal individualism, for her argument is also deeply preoccupied with debates about evolution, eugenics and maternity. This has worried later feminist commentators who regret that social Darwinism and forms of biological essentialism 'radically attenuate[ed] her political vision'.[12] But though it uses biological and evolutionary ideas *Woman and Labour* does not endorse eugenics or social Darwinism; rather it engages with these arguments in order to neutralize what Schreiner saw as their pernicious implications for women. Schreiner believed evolution was a powerful and truthful account of life and she was not prepared to cede it to politically regressive opponents.

Industrialization and technological innovation have definitively ended traditional patterns of labour, Schreiner contends in *Woman and Labour*. In response to the new demands of modern economies male labour expands into skilled technical, bureaucratic and scientific areas but, by contrast, female labour diminishes.[13] In particular, modern societies require fewer but more effectively (and 'professionally') educated children so that even child-bearing and rearing no longer necessarily occupy women's lives. Unlike men, who have no choice but to find new forms of labour as these changes occur, women have a dangerous alternative. They can become 'sex-parasites', a condition synonymous in Schreiner's account with the leisured idleness and conspicuous consumption of bourgeois femininity. In this state of parasitism, women support themselves not by productive economic activity but by their actual (or, worse, potential) 'sex function' in marriage or in prostitution (*WL* 71–7).

Drawing on her much-loved sources about the classical world – Edward Gibbon's *History of the Decline and Fall of the Roman Empire* (1776–88), Benjamin Jowett's translations of Plato and Theodor Mommsen's *History of Rome* (1854–6) – Schreiner identifies cultural, social and imperial decay throughout the past with elite and privileged classes. Dedicated to consumption, their 'possession of the results of the *labour of others'* inevitably leads to physical, mental and moral debilitation (*WL* 100). Because women can trade sexuality for economic support (as 'effete wife, concubine, or prostitute' (*WL* 81)), it is 'almost invariably' they who first succumb to this dangerous condition of dependency on others (*WL* 101–2). Schreiner's 'parasitism' thesis thus solders together as twin evils the trading of female sexuality and unearned wealth under capitalism. They are the real seeds of degeneration and decay and have debilitating effects for the wider social group.

The 'increasingly perfected labour-saving machinery' of modern economies, allied with rising support for the 'family wage' amongst socialists and trade unionists, means that female parasitism now risks infecting the working classes as well as middle classes: it 'threatens vast masses, and may, under future conditions, threaten the entire [social] body' (WL 115). Schreiner's argument here differs sharply from that of some of her socialist friends, such as Eleanor Marx, who believed that the economic transformations of socialism would inevitably produce the conditions for women's emancipation. Schreiner instead emphasizes the dangers of the socialist call for a family wage: gender relations are integral to how class is conceptualized for the greatest threat to the whole social body, she insists, is a structure which allows, encourages or requires women's dependency. Biological heredity means that if women are permitted or compelled into sex parasitism, the entire society is at risk: 'It is the woman who is the final standard of the race...as her brain weakens, weakens the man's she bears...as she decays, decays the people, (WL 109). Leisured femininity, far from signalling the conditions of advanced civilization, as argued by some evolutionary theorists like Herbert Spencer, is in fact 'the death-bed of human evolution' (WL 133).

But Schreiner also draws on the same examples from classical civilizations – those provided by Mommsen in particular – to provide an alternative to this bleak vision of female sexuality as associated with passivity, dependency and decay. History shows another model of femininity which she provocatively calls 'virile' womanhood. It is exemplified by 'that old, old Teutonic womanhood...that Brynhild whom Segurd found, clad in helm and byrne, the warrior maid' (WL 144–5). Modern 'New Women' are not in fact 'new' at all, but later manifestations of this energetic 'Teutonic' femininity. Schreiner is here mobilizing mid-Victorian ideas about the Teutonism of the English. Self-reliance and the dignity of labour were central features of English masculinity which are now appropriated for women.[14] As Emma Francis points out, however, Schreiner's insistence that women were originally (and 'naturally') labourers led her

41

to valorize ancient societies which were characterized by a rigid sexual division of labour: 'Man fought – that was his work; we fed and nurtured the race – that was ours' (*WL* 35).[15] But her argument for modern women depends on establishing that, under new conditions of technological modernity, labour can no longer be so divided. Metaphors of virility and the 'battlefield' work to bridge this gap, reducing division and difference between the sexes. While such images proved useful for the suffrage movement (which made ideas of battle and female heroism central to its campaigns) they are difficult for later readers – not least because of similar rhetoric later used in European fascism.

Schreiner herself was worried that her parasitism thesis would be misunderstood, explaining in the Introduction to *Woman and Labour* that it originally filled only one chapter of twelve before the manuscript was destroyed in the Anglo-Boer War. Its problematic rhetorical strategies and polemical targets only really come into focus in the context in which the original 'sex book' ideas emerged. In 1885 Schreiner was recruited to a newly formed discussion group in London called the Men and Women's Club that aimed to study gender and sexuality from a scientific viewpoint.[16] She responded enthusiastically to the Club's agenda and especially to the 'mental stimulation and strength' she discovered in its founder, the mathematician, socialist (and later eugenicist), Karl Pearson (*OSL* 116).[17] Relishing Pearson's demand for rigorous scientific methods and his outspoken criticisms and challenges, Schreiner was strongly attracted to him. However, complicated and criss-crossing desires and loyalties amongst members of the Club swiftly led to emotional turmoil and Schreiner became seriously ill. She departed England for the Continent where she spent most of 1887 and 1888. After a few months in London in the summer of 1889, she returned to South Africa in the autumn of that year. Her relationship with Pearson ended painfully – with Schreiner admitting that she loved him, but denying that the attraction was sexual, something Pearson clearly doubted (*OSL* 117). Nevertheless, he remained a powerful real and imagined intellectual interlocutor and antagonist. An aggressive proponent of the ideals of scientific enquiry to which Schreiner felt passionately committed, he also exemplified how science was no guarantee of 'impersonal' truth but could be put to uses with which she fundamentally disagreed.

Pearson believed that any future evolutionary progress for modern societies depended on the subordination of individual wishes to the needs of the social whole. His interpretation and political appropriation of biological evolutionary ideas thus contrasted sharply with Herbert Spencer's, for example. Spencer's influential social Darwinism emphasized the individual. Competitive capitalism distinguished between the 'fittest', who could flourish, and the weak who failed. Laissez-faire economics was seen to facilitate this process, while social welfare was deemed socially damaging because it hindered evolutionary progress by protecting society's weakest members. Spencer believed that 'advanced' societies, employing welfare measures, dangerously disabled 'natural' selection.[18] Pearson also believed that natural selection no longer functioned in modern society but he strongly opposed Spencer's individualistic model. Instead, he argued that the struggle and competition of the Darwinian world would be replaced in modern societies by external national and racial contest. Internal 'fitness' would be managed by the state, through 'insuring that its numbers are substantially recruited from the better stocks'.[19] Natural selection would give way to the 'rational' selection espoused by eugenicists.

Women's social duty for Pearson and other eugenic enthusiasts is as child-bearers for the future of the race and the nation. Any movement into other types of activity (education or employment) must be strictly overseen to ensure no conflict arises with this primary duty of maternity. The combination of social duty and the primacy of reason was an attractive one for many feminists, and New Woman novelists such as Sarah Grand popularized images of 'modern' women for whom love, sex and marriage were matters of rational decision-making rather than convention or emotion.[20] For Pearson, 'healthy' women who fulfil the 'high social function' of childbirth and childrearing should be protected from the competitive economic marketplace by the provision of state support for their maternity.[21] This was a prospect which horrified Schreiner, who believed that it would re-entrench women's economic dependency, and her parasitism thesis in *Woman and Labour* aims to show that 'maternity' separated from other types of productive labour is dangerous for women *and* for men.

Woman and Labour thus tries to combat eugenic versions of female morality and social progress by retelling evolutionary human history as the story of work – but one told from the seldom-heard female point of view.[22] Schreiner's occasionally contradictory arguments about sexuality and maternity are a result of her attempt to fuse together evolutionary teleology and the epic values of classical and Biblical history. By demonstrating that women have always undertaken 'our share of honoured and socially useful toil', Schreiner seeks to establish 'labouring' as women's natural and original condition (*WL* 68). At the same time, she also contends that women's propensity to dependency based on their reproductive function ('sex-parasitism') is so historically prevalent that it too seems 'natural'. To manage this tension, she creates an opposition between active production and passive reproduction. Augmented by other kinds of work, child-bearing (reproduction) is transformed into production (of 'the race') and correspondingly valued. But unsupported by other types of work, it is 'passive labour', a passivity which turns sexuality into consumption rather than production. Schreiner characterizes this as a cycle of decline which leads from women who bear children but do little of the work of raising them, to women who are economically supported because of their sexuality and bear few or no children. From here, it is a short step to prostitution, and the prostitute metaphorically closes the circle by becoming productive once more – but, 'in place of life, is recognised as producing death and disease' (*WL* 116, 104). Schreiner's argument thus evokes and uses for feminist purposes images of degeneration which were widespread at the end of the century.

Emma Francis has noted that *Woman and Labour* rewrites the Biblical Genesis but the 'fall' Schreiner describes is out of the Eden of 'productive social labour'.[23] William Morris had made the values of communal production in labour and aesthetics central to his socialist critique of modern capitalism. His 'aesthetics of manly labour' were a counter to the so-called decadent aestheticism of the 1880s and 1890s which emphasized individual consumption. These virtues of 'manly' artistry and labour, as Ruth Livesey shows, were widely adopted and revised by socialist women, and are incorporated by Schreiner into the image of active 'virile' womanhood.[24] Schreiner had a very close friendship with Edward Carpenter (providing sympathetic support during vicissitudes in his same-sex love relationships), a good working relationship with Oscar Wilde (who edited the *Woman's World* between 1887 and 1890, where Schreiner published a number of allegories) and judged Vernon Lee 'one of the most valuable women we have'.[25] In the light of these relationships, *Woman and Labour*'s condemnation of the 'effeminate' aesthete man, the 'curled darling, scented and languid' seems especially shocking (*WL* 107). It is, however, more explicable in the wider context of labour and value: as Livesey argues, the aesthete man 'is a metonym of a society – and crucially an aesthetic – that is founded on parasitic consumption rather than labouring production'.[26]

In addition, Schreiner's metaphor of parasitism borrows from a popularly used illustration of evolutionary forces at work in nature which showed that evolution – natural or social – is not necessarily progressive but can be degenerative (*WL* fn. 77–8). Socialists like H. G. Wells (who as a student studied science under Thomas Henry Huxley, the man known as 'Darwin's Bulldog' for his robust public advocacy of evolution) evoked fears of a downward evolutionary spiral in which once active organisms are reduced to 'vegetative excrescence[s] on a rock' as a means to attack the non-productive, over-consuming members of British society's highest social classes.[27]

Fears about national and racial decline had gathered momentum during the second half of the nineteenth century. Although Britain was indisputably wealthy and powerful, with an empire which expanded across the globe, the rhetoric of national progress and civilization sat uncomfortably with abundant evidence of extreme poverty and degradation.[28] Social investigations, pamphlets and new forms of popular journalism publicized and disseminated images of 'outcast' London, a place as strange and alien to 'respectable' Britain as 'darkest Africa'.[29] Max Nordau's sensationalist *Degeneration*, which appeared in English in 1895, announced the encroaching 'Dusk of Nations', and lamented a widespread cultural degeneracy in Europe. Oscar Wilde's fall in the same year from fêted author to convicted felon seemed to some telling confirmation of Nordau's treatise. By the end of the decade, eugenic enthusiasts pounced on fears about the decline of 'national stock' as confirmation of their ideas. These fears reached fever pitch as a consequence of Britain's humiliating defeats at the hands of the Boers in South Africa in the first months of the war which began in 1899.[30]

Schreiner (who was writing *Woman and Labour* during this war) was determined that fears about racial and national decline and degeneration in Britain should not conflict with or undermine women's calls for equality and autonomy. Degeneration was not a consequence of middle-class women refusing to have children, and nor should the state support child-bearing. Instead, Schreiner made economically dependent maternity itself synonymous with degeneration, and projected mythologized, epic history as a model for a re-valued future maternity. She was, though, well aware that focusing so much on maternity skewed the picture. In the Introduction to *Woman and Labour* (which she wrote around 1909), she reminded readers that her original plans included an argument about the re-valuing of paternity too: over one hundred pages of the original work destroyed in Johannesburg focused on men's role in raising their children. Equal pay for equal work, and appropriate recognition and recompense of domestic labour, were further issues of 'vital importance' discussed in the original work (*WL* 24–5). There is also the hint of a different vision of sexuality. This sexuality is defiantly *not* circumscribed by biology: it extends far beyond maternity and suggests self-realization rather than self-sacrifice. It is only our 'present barbarous and semi-savage condition in matters of sex', Schreiner insists, that distorts the 'distinct aesthetic, intellectual, and spiritual functions and ends' of sexual relations. Physical reproduction is not the only, or indeed the highest, aim of sex. The history of its 'creative energy and life-dispensing power...has only begun' (*WL* 27).

But in *Woman and Labour* Schreiner found it impossible to incorporate this ideal of sexuality and self-realization into her narratives of history and change. The evolutionary languages she used were powerful and enabling, but were also capable of being alarmingly reductive, something Schreiner sought to resist by turning to aesthetics. Although she believed passionately that modern science was a progressive force she was increasingly dismayed at how it was used to shore up injustice and consolidate existing power structures. She also believed that habitual oppositions associated with 'objective' thought (between, for example, intellect and feeling) were damaging and mistaken. In the mid-1880s she warned Pearson that 'the child of exact knowledge' they were rearing with such care may swell 'into a giant' and have in turn to be combated (*OSL* 111). Her own form of combat was her experimentation with allegory. As Liz Stanley notes: 'her aesthetics are less about questions of ethics than they *are* her ethics; or, rather, her ethics and her aesthetics are each constitutive of the other'.[31] This is nowhere clearer than in the numerous short fictions Schreiner wrote during the 1880s and early 1890s.

DREAMING THE FUTURE: ALLEGORIES AND STORIES

Schreiner's collection of allegorical fictions, entitled *Dreams*, was published at the end of 1890, at the outset of the decade which saw the high-point of aestheticism. They were championed by Arthur Symons, a leading supporter of the literary 'Decadent' movement. He wrote a long account of Schreiner, commenting on her allegories: 'all art is a symbol and these are pure symbol themselves – the only artistic expression of the passion of abstract ideas' (*LiOS* 185). Reviewing *Dreams* in 1891, he describes the allegories as 'a daring experiment in the direction of a more vocal prose', entranced by how they evoke both image and music: 'the words seem to chant themselves to a music which we do not hear'.[32] For Schreiner, they exemplified a literary method that was antithetic to the rationalism and valorization of objectivity dominating late nineteenth-century scientific culture. She frequently described the allegories as having been worked out unconsciously, and then suddenly 'flashing' on her consciousness: 'Three Dreams in a Desert', for example, came to her while she was in Paris, walking on a bridge over the river Seine, 'when suddenly all flashed upon her. She screamed aloud, and began to run . . . and ran till she came to her lodgings, when she sat down and never rose till the allegory was finished' (*LiOS* 189). In method and in content the allegories evoke, question and trouble dominant forms of social understanding. The universalizing

47

mode of allegory also reveals sharp tensions about modernization when inflected through the lens of colonial experience. In these allegories, the position of women was not separable from other forms of dominance and subjection.

In allegory Schreiner could telescope the 'monumental time scale' of evolution for women, encapsulating the past, present and future.[33] This is explicitly done in 'Three Dreams in a Desert' which, Schreiner explains in the Introduction of *Woman and Labour*, was originally planned as part of her 'sex book' (*WL* fn. 16). The first of the three dreams (the past) echoes the theme of the evolutionary inevitability of women's historic subjection on which *Woman and Labour* focuses. The dreamer looks onto a desert and sees two great figures, one bound to the ground and each to the other. An unidentified interlocutor explains that the bound figure is woman whom the 'Age-of-dominion-of-muscular-force' had immobilized with the band of 'Inevitable Necessity'. But the band cracks and breaks as 'Mechanical Invention' severs it in the triumph of the 'Age-of-nervous-force'. The woman struggles to move but is weak from centuries of stillness. The man beside her is bound to her and cannot move without her – but nor can he help her, the dreamer is told. She must struggle alone until she is strong enough to stagger to her knees (*D*. 71–3).

As in *Woman and Labour*, history is an ineluctable and determinist evolutionary process rather than human-shaped. The woman's agency is born at this moment, on what Scott McCracken has characterized as a 'stage' for the performance of New Womanhood's emergent subjectivity. The moral landscape of the desert – signifying archaic human origins – is mediated through the narrative frame in which the dreamer rests (and dreams) under a mimosa tree in an African landscape of fierce heat and red sand. The dream landscape is thus both abstract/ allegoric and African, a literary device which inserts the conditions of colonialism into the story of women's emancipation.[34] Laura Chrisman sees the African desert as a source of narrative ambiguity. The oscillation between a mythic desert origin of humankind, a specifically African stage of subjection, and Western technological modernity, creates tension for the universal ideal of liberation, complicating the focus on gender and implicating women in other oppressions.[35]

The second dream takes place in a landscape specifically identified as African. A woman comes out of the desert to an African river, steep and high-banked and very deep (*D*. 75). She is searching for the land of Freedom and is guided by an old man, Reason, who tells her that she must descend the steep banks of Labour and cross the deep waters of Suffering by a path she must make herself. Before starting she must shed the trappings of convention and dependence to be clad only in the white garment of Truth. More painfully, she must also give up the small winged creature whom she has long carried hidden in her breast. He lisps one word, 'Passion', and she dreams of him saying 'friendship' in the Land of Freedom (*D*. 76–80).

Here, in the present, the female figure has agency: she must choose Reason over Passion (sexual love). As she relinquishes the creature in her breast, however, it bites her so that blood runs to the ground and, as she turns away, the dreamer sees 'the hair on her forehead turned white as snow, and she had changed from youth to age' (*D*. 81). The cost of attaining selfhood is enormous, and the woman's plea for her individuality is only answered by the knowledge that she suffers for '*The entire human race*' who will follow the path she makes (*D*. 83; Schreiner's emphasis). The allegory is derived from Biblical imagery from both Old and New Testaments: Exodus, the myth of deliverance, and the founding of a new land, sit alongside images of the desert in which Christ hungers, and intimations of a suffering followed by resurrection.

Reassuring her that her lonely striving will not be fruitless, Reason evokes an image of a natural collectivity, reminding the woman of locusts crossing water whose bodies form a bridge over which 'the rest pass over'. This biological analogy turns the drama of individuation towards the vision of the third dream – the future. No longer a desert, this is a 'heaven' of heterosexual and same-sex couples living in utopian-socialist harmony. It is both a collective and a distinctly material heaven – it is 'On earth' (*D*. 84). But the utopian energies of this third brief allegoric scene are again bound by the frame narrative. The dreamer wakes for a final time to a landscape which is rapidly cooling: 'Then the sun passed down behind the hills; but I knew that the next day he would rise again' (*D*. 85). McCracken has pointed to the 'shock' effect of the masculine pronoun in the final phrase. The conventional sense of a new day is troubled by the suggestion of a resurgent masculine force which acts as a reminder of the current state of colonial and gender relations which remain, as yet, unchanged.[36] It is as if the allegory both advocates and, at the same time, registers the problems of, the evolutionary story it dramatizes.

The relation between aesthetics and idealism is the focus of an allegory which Schreiner wrote in London in the mid-1880s and sent in a letter to Karl Pearson. In 'A Dream of Wild Bees' a woman heavily pregnant with her ninth child sits sewing. A book, signalling the woman's snatched intellectual life, is at her side. Lulled to sleep by the sonorous humming of bees she dreams that the buzzing drones – 'the long-legged wasp-like fellows who make no honey' – turn into men offering futures for her unborn child. Health, wealth, fame, love and talent are all refused by the mother until the last, who questions 'What *is* real?' and bequeaths to the unborn child the capacity to know that reality is shaped and formed by ideals: '*This shall be thy reward – that the ideal shall be real to thee*' (D. 90, 96; Schreiner's emphasis). Reality is not fixed or given by biology or any other physical law but is shaped by human ideals to be realized through exertion, creativity and hope.

The bee-life depicted in this tiny allegory to Pearson complicates and overturns the organization of male production and female reproduction central to his eugenics. In folk history drones are named for their 'idling'. Unlike the honey-making worker bee, their function is reproductive, and in the allegory they gather around the pregnant woman as round a queen bee. This mother does indeed determine the future of her unborn child, as eugenicists insisted was the case. But she does so by her wisdom, and her commitment to hope, not by her biology. Procreation is not only material race reproduction, nor is it a mechanistic and rational process of citizen-making. Instead, maternal imagination turns physical birth into the birth of hope and makes hope the condition of life itself.[37] As the mother makes her choice for the unborn child in her womb it receives a sensation of light: 'Light – that it had never seen. Light – that perhaps it never should see. Light – that existed somewhere!' (D. 96).

Unlike the accounts Schreiner gives of other kinds of writing, she invariably referred to these allegories and 'dreams' as if they were visited on her from elsewhere, or the products of a kind of distraction and dictation: 'With all these dreams coming I never get to any other work. Can't help it – they *will* come', she wrote to Ellis, lamenting that 'my friends pitch into me when I make dreams about God. I can't help it, they come'.[38] The notion of dream-states as providing privileged access to psychic interiority was an important feature of emergent psychological discourse across the century, discussed in scientific works such as George Henry Lewes's *Physiology of Common Life* (1859) and popular tracts such as Catherine Crowe's *The Night-Side of Nature* (1848). By the final decades of the century, the notion of a psyche divided between consciousness and an unconscious realm was widely debated, and proved a powerful spur for experimental artistic and literary work seeking to disrupt or see beyond what was experienced as a rigid and restrictive materialism. Associated notions of hitherto undiscovered 'occult' phenomena were widely investigated. Schreiner was friendly with the journalist W. T. Stead, a keen advocate of spiritualism who launched a quarterly periodical devoted to spiritualism in 1893, and practiced 'automatic writing'. Havelock Ellis wrote in the *Contemporary Review* in 1898 of the drug mescal, announcing himself as the first Briton to experiment with its 'vision-producing properties'.[39] Psychic experience is the inner side of the material changes Schreiner advocated and apprehending it necessitated a different kind of writing. Its implications for agency and for politics were far-reaching, presaging the emphasis in the later-twentieth-century women's movement that 'the personal is political'.

Some of the allegories – such as 'In a Far-Off World', which features a woman who loses her lover – thus focus on the affective transformations that Schreiner believed must accompany material change. Arguing about sexual passion with Pearson in the mid-1880s, Schreiner was emphatic that emotional and sexual selves are not givens, determined by biology or instinct: 'There is nothing in which the race develops so much as in its affections'. The 'old, cruel sensual "You must be mine! I will win your love though you die for it. I will tear you to pieces but I must *have* you!"', must be replaced. The sexual feelings she imagines for the future may be completely new, she admits, 'and so are the electric telegraph and the steam-ship; but they are not less real for that' (*OSL* 75). Given her feelings for Pearson at the time she wrote this, her comments are poignant, but they also underline her resistance to the deterministic account of sexual selection found in Darwin's *Descent of Man* (1871). Emotional and sexual life must change alongside social and material transformation: they are not biologically fixed.

Writing to Pearson after their friendship had ended, Schreiner acknowledged how he helped her stem a recklessly open sympathy for others in espousing 'self-consciousness and self-concentration'. Likening him to ice applied to a bleeding wound, she admitted that time spent listening to other women's woes, or providing prostitutes with a temporary haven in her lodgings, or writing long letters, fearful of having hurt someone, all interrupted her writing. But she also insisted on the indispensable value of identificatory sympathy: 'Those women taught me what I could not otherwise have learnt. I would not have those years blotted out. They are my most precious heritage' (*OSL* 179). This unquantifiable, often ambivalent, quality of feeling for others was central to Schreiner's politics and aesthetics. It is the focus of the allegory, 'I Thought I Stood' in which a woman stands before God's throne to arraign men. She accuses them of having blood on their hands because of their sexual mistreatment of women. She shows God her own white hands but God points to her feet, which are blood-red, and she explains how "'the streets on earth are full of mire. If I should walk straight on in them my outer robe might be bespotted, you see how white it is! Therefore I pick my way." God said "*On what?*'"(*D.* 126). The woman realizes that she, too, is complicit in the economic and social structures which produce poverty and prostitution. Middle-class women's emancipation cannot be gained at the cost of other women's degradation, and identification must be able to cross the borders of class, status and race. There is a large political argument in this small story.

Sympathy, identification and feeling for others are necessary human capacities but how they are exercised is contingent and political. 'The Woman's Rose', one of the tiny stories which appeared in 1893 in *Dream Life and Real Life*, dramatizes how two women are positioned as sexual rivals. In her reading of this story, Laura Chrisman notes that the target of Schreiner's narration is a 'colonial structure...in which settler colonialism, sexual commercialism and capitalist economics are inextricable'. The women are able to perform and prefigure 'a radical alternative'.[40] In the story, a colonial town is largely populated by single men who lay bets on which of the two is prettier – underlining how the women are commodified as sexual objects. Constructed as rivals, they have no other means of relating to each other until, in the waiting-room before a party, the fair-haired woman unpins a precious and rare rose from her own hair and replaces it in the narrator's. The narrator watches this subversive gift-giving refracted through a mirror. The women can then look at each other fully, for the first time, apart from the men's valuations: 'You are so beautiful to me', the narrator says. 'I'm so glad', the other woman replies, in an exchange of aesthetic, erotic and subjective affirmation which – momentarily at least – frees them from the competition and calculation of the colonial marriage market (*DLRL* 63).

The compressed and metaphoric qualities of allegory defused the moralism associated with suffering, loss and renunciation, replacing exhortatory rhetoric with an unsentimental spare beauty. Their lyrical images allowed Schreiner to fuse future utopian hopefulness and present conditions. Allegory also freed her to suggest connections – ones often deriving from the desert settings of the stories – between a symbolic land and the real, if far-off, places where other types of exploitation occur. The poetic, often Biblical cadence lent the stories parable-like clarity which dissolved the distance between ideal and reality. Constance Lytton recalled 'Three Dreams in a Desert' being read aloud to imprisoned suffragettes by Emmeline Pethick-Lawrence, claiming that it 'seemed scarcely an allegory...It fell on our ears more like an A B C railway guide to our journey than a figurative parable'.[41]

Nevertheless, when *Dreams* appeared, towards the end of 1890, most reviewers were disappointed that Schreiner had not provided a second novel to follow *The Story of an African Farm*. Schreiner worked intermittently in the 1880s on her 'big' novel *From Man to Man*. The topic of prostitution, so important to her thinking during the decade, is at its heart. She did not complete it, however, and took the manuscript with her when she returned to South Africa in 1889. The feminist story Schreiner aimed to tell in *From Man to Man* became complicated as a result of South Africa in ways she did not anticipate earlier in the decade. Her novel changed as she struggled to find a way to represent sexual inequality as it became complicated by other types of social injustice – and most obviously the issue of race.

DESIRE AND PEDAGOGY: *FROM MAN TO MAN*

On 7 June 1889 London's Novelty Theatre staged the first full production of Henrik Ibsen's *A Doll's House*. Intellectuals and radicals flocked to see it, amongst them Schreiner, Eleanor Marx, Dolly Radford, George Bernard Shaw, and Edith Lees, the woman Havelock Ellis was eventually to marry. Lees remembered some of them gathering excitedly after the performance: 'We were restive and almost savage in our arguments. What did it mean?...Was it life or death for women?'[42] The famous slamming of the door at the play's end, announcing Nora Helmer's desertion of her husband and children, reverberated through Victorian fin-de-siècle culture and inaugurated a dramatic change in the traditional Victorian marriage plot. The most popular and talked-about novels of the following decade were by New Women, for whom marriage was not a satisfactory terminus in the narrative of bourgeois femininity, but the starting point for a thoroughgoing critique of gender relations, sexual double standards and Victorian morality. Waves of condemnation ensued in the periodical press, illustrated by the critic who saw the 'socialistic Nora' as 'the apostle of the new creed of humanity... It is all self, self, self!'[43]

Of all Schreiner's writing *From Man to Man* comes closest to being a 'New Woman' text, especially in its contrast between an 'advanced' and a more traditionally feminine woman, and its focus on the pitfalls of love and marriage. The plot links the lives of two sisters: the elder, Rebekah, is intense and intellectual while Bertie is sweet, innocent-minded, loving and very beautiful. Rebekah spells out the dangers confronting women such as Bertie who 'have only one life possible, the life of the personal relations; if that fails them all fails' (*FMM* 121). In the novel's dense imagery, which meshes together religious and scientific meanings, Rebekah is likened to a mimosa tree which, though chopped in its main stem, can still eventually shoot new life and even flower. Bertie, however, is imagined as the aloe that bears one flower and once cut down never again blooms (*FMM* 121–2).[44] This cataclysmically restricted feminine life unfolds as a bleak echo of the Victorian 'fallen woman' narrative. Bertie is seduced by her tutor and, as a consequence, rejected by the suitor with whom she falls in love. Thereafter, she moves restlessly around the Cape, pursued by the gossip of envious women until she is taken to London as a kept mistress and from there descends into life as a street prostitute.

Schreiner told Pearson that she intended none of the men who help seal Bertie's fate to be represented as 'depraved', but merely ordinary in seeing 'woman as a creature created entirely for their benefit' (*OSL* 91). As she originally conceived the novel the force of its feminist critique derives from the fact that Bertie's career is mirrored by her sister's. Rebekah, married to her cousin, Frank, painfully comes to see her own state as little better than legalized prostitution, tied to a sexually philandering man whose infidelities and betrayals destroy everything marriage means to her: 'Oh, it isn't only the body of a woman that a man touches when he takes her in his hands; it's her brain, it's her intellect, it's her whole life!', Rebekah laments (*FMM* 273). Marriage boils down to a contract where sexual and domestic services are traded for economic security.

Marxist theorists such as Friedrich Engels argued that bourgeois marriage is the mechanism by which capitalism transmits property, with women effectively serving an economic system. He provocatively asserted that the bourgeois wife differs from the prostitute only inasmuch as the latter lets out her body as 'a wage worker', while marriage amounts to being sold 'once and for all into slavery'.[45] W. E. Lecky, in a book Schreiner read at the end of the 1870s, the *History of European Morals from Augustus to Charlemagne* (1869), argued that sensual passion in excess of reproductive needs was an 'original sin' of human nature, and prostitution thus a necessary vice which protected families and homes.[46] Schreiner sought to tackle both arguments. In *From Man to Man* women's maintaining economic independence in marriage is as important a first step as it is in *Woman and Labour*. Schreiner had ticked off her friend Edward Carpenter for writing an essay that did not 'dwell QUITE enough on the monetary independence of women as the first condition necessary to the putting of things on the right footing' (*OSL* 241). But *From Man to Man* is equally an exploration of sexual desire itself. Unlike some of the 'social purity' feminists of the period, Schreiner believed moral strictures about sexual abstinence were foolish. She vehemently disagreed with the orthodox belief in women's relative lack of sexual passion emphasized by physicians such as William Acton, and she opposed feminists who presented female sexual continence as a sign of women's superior morality. Rebekah's characterization may also be a riposte to the eugenic arguments already encountered in *Woman and Labour* – especially Pearson's charge that feminists were by definition more interested in public than in domestic and familial affairs and, as a result, would bear fewer children, gradually rendering their 'type' obsolete.

For Schreiner's most fully-realized feminist protagonist, Rebekah, is a very domestic New Woman. In the small house in a Cape Town suburb where she lives with her husband Rebekah gives birth to four sons, and adopts another child. She plants a flower garden edged by a blooming rose hedge. She kneads bread, makes salads, cleans windows and mends clothes. As mentioned earlier, Schreiner called *From Man to Man*, 'the most womanly book that ever was written', adding, 'and God knows that I've willed it otherwise!' (*OSL* 149). But 'womanliness' is shown to be a complex, not a singular, identity. Of the two sisters, Bertie is most beautiful, feminine and domestic: her femininity is stereotypic whereas Rebekah's is more unusual. Rebekah's domestic 'private sphere' – a tiny space made by partitioning off a section of her children's bedroom – is the place where she reads, thinks and writes. It is intensely feminine – she darns there, her lower body and legs aching in the stages of early pregnancy – *and* also intellectual. Here, she makes fragmentary personal diary entries about her marriage and conducts long impersonal Socratic discussions with herself about religion, evolution, social progress, art and relations between the sexes. Her probing, investigative mental life – evidence of evolved humankind, as Rose Lovell-Smith points out – takes place in the midst of (and perhaps because of) her practical domesticity and mothering.[47]

Rebekah is also a mother-scientist, examining the natural world under her microscope and the human world through her affective imagination and intellectual enquiry. An informed and passionate advocate of evolution she is equally its critic. The universe imagined by social Darwinism as dominated by struggle, competition and destruction, is challenged by her evolutionary alternatives. She resists ideas of human hierarchy, dismantling arguments about 'fitness', and asking who are the real criminals that eugenicists seek to stamp out (FMM 199–200). In place of the so-called 'natural law' of grim evolutionary struggle she offers 'love and the expansion of the ego to others' as the highest evolved state. The exemplary model of this love is maternity: 'through all nature, life and growth and evolution are possible because of mother-love' (FMM 209–10). But Rebekah's 'mother-love' is not a naturalistic or essentialist category. It is a self-conscious counter-ethics which can (and must) be a quality of men as much as women. Thus her examples of 'mother-love' are of males of different animal species. They culminate with an image which evokes an alternative Darwinism: illustrating the social nature of instinctual life, she recalls watching a male baboon defend its troop of females and young from dogs that tear him to pieces. It is an obvious echo of the almost identical scene of 'an old baboon' confronting a dog to rescue one of its young which is used by Darwin when he famously affirms his descent from primate creatures at the conclusion of The Descent of Man (1871).[48]

This revised Darwinism, in effect a feminist theory of evolution, provides Rebekah with an ethical basis for her life. It enables her to understand and analyse the obduracy of her desire for her husband, Frank. In the long letter she writes to him after discovering that he is having sex with the young coloured servant who helps Rebekah in the house, she describes sexual love as a lure-light or decoy which 'leads women on to surrender and bear for men'. Even though she has learned through repeated bitter experience that Frank's desire is treacherous and casual – she has seen him turn to other women, 'plain it might be, with the same passionate light in your eyes begging for a return of sexual feeling, which you once turned on me' – she acknowledges the force and power of that desire. 'Oh, now, even now, when I know what it means, something in me cries out to see it once more, my light, for me, just once before I die!' (FMM 287, 296).

The idea that sexual love can be made 'rational', as proposed by eugenicists, was as misguided in Schreiner's view as the notion that intellectual women were less likely to desire sexual fulfilment and motherhood. Rebekah acknowledges and affirms sexuality's biological and instinctual roots: far from moralizing about sexual appetite she insists that 'I can understand, I can almost sympathise with, a wave of black, primitive bestial desire surging up' (FMM 287). But to be without any internal ethical guide to check such feeling is to be blighted and not properly human. It would be like living in a land 'that always trembled, that was never still, when from every smallest crack the foetid fume rose, and a fine, almost imperceptible, fall of ashes covered it: the very dogs would leave it – no man would live there!' (FMM 28).[49] Rebekah's analysis pits her own version of civilization as other-oriented affective sociality ('love and the expansion of ego to others') against a vision as desolate as the degenerate world of the far-distant future described by H. G. Wells' Time Traveller, populated by giant crabs and algal slime.[50]

But this leaves some serious narrative problems. Schreiner was well aware that dramatizing Rebekah's isolated and hard-won insights was a tough task. She asked Cronwright to say honestly of one chapter whether he found it interesting, and admitted that Rebekah could not have written her letter to Frank in the space of one night (LOS 279). Novelistic realism proved a difficult medium to represent the quiet inner transformation that dominates Rebekah's story. Within the story, too, all Rebekah's insight and critique – her journal writing and her letter to her husband Frank – remains private, undertaken and confined in the tiny space of her study. Frank calls the letter to him a book and refuses to read it. Schreiner alerts us to the irony here by calling the chapter 'You Cannot Capture the Ideal by a Coup D'Etat'. The irony intensifies when, at the end of her long disquisition on social Darwinism, Rebekah fantasizes about being a man and falls asleep dreaming of being able 'to take care of and defend all the creatures weaker and smaller than you are' (FMM 226). She is woken by a slamming door but fails to see anything when she investigates. She thus misses the fact that Bertie has run home from a dance because of malicious gossip: in contrast to Rebekah and her intense inner experience, Bertie is constantly forced into desperate external action. The gossip at the dance hounds her away from safety and there is no help from Rebekah. Shut up in her private room, Rebekah's fantasy of being able to care for and defend others remains just that.

However, while Bertie's narrative is characterized by melodrama and caricature, Schreiner remains resolutely committed to depicting Rebekah's undramatic transformation. Unlike Ibsen's Nora, she does not leave her home when she reaches crisis-point, on discovering that her husband Frank's coloured mistress is pregnant with his child. As Liz Stanley puts it, Rebekah 'does not so much rebel' as find 'moral authority within herself'.[51] The process is symbolized not by rejection of family and domesticity but by the latter's (small-scale) material transformation. After a break in Rebekah's narrative (we rejoin her story after a gap of five years) we learn that her study door is sealed off and new rooms have been built in the yard. Rebekah supports herself economically by the proceeds of a small landholding which she farms. She caters for Frank's material needs but not his sexual or emotional ones, and shares her new room with her adopted daughter, Sartje, the child born illegitimately to Frank. These are the slow processes of personal evolution in contrast to the revolutionary door-slamming of Ibsen's New Woman drama.

There is evidence to suggest that Schreiner developed the plot about Sartje, Rebekah's adopted daughter, late in *From Man to Man*'s genesis. Liz Stanley believes that she last worked on the novel in 1907, and her diary from February of that year records that she completed the chapter in which Rebekah discovers that Frank has fathered an illegitimate child (*LiOS* 350).[52] She also wrote in 1908 to Cronwright asking him to read the chapter which focuses on Sartje (*LOS* 279). The long account of the novel she sent to Karl Pearson in 1886 contains no intimation at all of an adopted coloured child. Instead, this 1880s sketch focuses primarily on Rebekah's relationship with the New Man, Mr Drummond (*OSL* 91–4). Sartje complicates the more straightforward New Woman plot with which Schreiner began. Her presence suggests that Schreiner felt a feminist narrative about the current malaise of sexual desire and relations between men and women could not be kept separate from the complications of her colonial context.

In making the target of Frank's sexual appetite a 'coloured servant-girl', Schreiner evokes a long history of sexual and racial exploitation. The Cape's 'Coloured' population (as it was called) originated as a complex grouping of indigenous Khoi and San peoples together with descendants of slaves and ex-slaves, many of whom were born of sexual relations between slave-owners and slave women or, more commonly, between white men and Dutch-speaking Cape-born women of mixed parentage.[53] Race dramatically signals the limit of Rebekah's tolerance of her husband's infidelities: she knows that adultery with a coloured or black woman gives her legal power in a divorce court, but she also affirms that, whatever the views of white community, her husband's sexual betrayal of her with a coloured woman is not different in her eyes to sex with white women (FMM 287). What *is* at last intolerable is that Frank's predatory desire is so casual, so irresponsible and so little different to the exploitative, slave-owning, past. His infidelities dramatize how sexual greed is an element of a much wider and deeper problem of power and abuse in colonial society. In 1911, participating in debate about the so-called 'Black Peril', when a commission investigated whether white women were at risk of rape and sexual violence from black men, Schreiner insisted that the real peril 'exists for all dark skinned women *at the hands of white men*' (Schreiner's emphasis).[54]

Schreiner's sense of the urgency of linking together women's emancipation with the wider issues of exploitation in colonial society certainly intensified after she returned to South Africa in 1889. But to over-emphasize this would be wrong as her colonial experience was always a fundamental part of Schreiner's imagination. In 1888, she wrote a 'Prelude' to From Man to Man called 'The Child's Day', 'a picture in small ... of the life of the woman in the book', set on the day on which the five-year-old Rebekah's sister Bertie is born (FMM 493). Excluded from the great events of birth and death (the new baby is one of twins, and the other is stillborn) taking place in the house, Rebekah imagines having her own baby. It becomes the recipient of her storytelling, bits and pieces patched together from the Bible, from English poetry and Dissenting songs and tales. These are the received materials of her culture, through which she struggles to make sense of her African world. They include

Byron's 'The Destruction of Sennacherib', an Indian Mutiny tale and William Cowper's 'Boadicea: an Ode'. Replete with themes of imperial power and domination, of missionaries and of motherhood, Rebekah tries to make them her own and pass them on. But important elements remain opaque to her. She quotes Cowper: "'Rome, for Empire far renown/Tramps on a thousand states" ... I could understand it all, except for "For-empire" and "far-renown." I don't know what "far-renown" is – or "for-empire'" (*FMM* 55). These are phrases that will eventually make sense for the grown-up Rebekah in relation to a South African context in which imperialism means exploitation and (sexual) violence.

This grown-up Rebekah's newly autonomous domestic space is where she now tells very different stories to her real children. Understanding what 'for-empire' means in the context of South Africa, she turns her own experience into a form of pedagogy for her children. Her political efficacy is still limited to the domestic rooms where she lives, but she is no longer isolated: instead, she teaches the next generation. Responding to an outburst from one of her sons who objects to having to walk in public beside his 'coloured' half-sister, Sartje, Rebekah recollects similar prejudice from her own childhood:

> I always played that I was Queen Victoria and that all Africa belonged to me, and I could do whatever I liked. It always puzzled me... what I should do with the black people; I did not like to kill them... and yet I could not have them near me. At last I made a plan. I made believe I built a high wall right across Africa and put all the black people on the other side, and I said, 'Stay there, and the day you put one foot over, your heads will be cut off.' (*FMM* 435)

Rebekah explains that overheard stories gradually helped her understand her common humanity with those around her, black and white – just as she intends her own stories to act as barriers to the racism threatening to influence her children. Listening to an account of a young African woman's bravery during a war with colonizers, or hearing gossip about a black woman who killed herself and her children in a state of grief occasioned by her husband's rejection, Rebekah imaginatively identified with them and 'the wall I had built across Africa had slowly to fall down' (*FMM* 438).

In her 1901 introduction to the essays she wrote in the 1890s on South Africa, Schreiner recalls the 'insular prejudice and racial pride' of her early years, admitting that the fantasized wall across Africa which Rebekah describes was originally her own invention (*TSA* 17). Writing at the beginning of the twentieth century, Schreiner could not have known how ominously prophetic her child's vision of a dividing wall would prove for the later history of South Africa. Apartheid – a term derived from the Afrikaans word for 'apartness' – was a real and terrible manifestation of that childish fantasy, one which dominated state policy in South Africa between 1948 and 1994. Schreiner's own childhood environment contained no maternal guidance like Rebekah's, however. Her mother, the main provider of Schreiner's education, despised what she deemed 'romantic' views of black people held by Europeans. She lamented the difficulty of keeping her children 'separate from the swarthy demon of the house', and made caustic references to 'pet blacks' (*WSA* 61, 95). In an endemically racist white culture, which offered only idealization or denigration in relation to the indigenous populations, Schreiner's developing critique of European claims to racial superiority was achieved against the grain of her family and social environment.

When Schreiner left South Africa for the first time in 1881 she dreamed of an expansive intellectual world, as different as possible from the culture of colonial South Africa. In England she was soon a literary celebrity, with a wide network of friendships amongst the men and women who were shaping the political and artistic climate of the decade. The socialist and feminist debates of these years lent shape to her vision of social justice but the distinctiveness of Schreiner's voice was forged in her experiences growing up in South Africa. She returned there in 1889 a little bruised by her romantic experiences and greatly enriched by some intellectual ones. In the years that followed she was struck by how serious, how terrible, history could prove to be. The final chapter examines how her writing changed as a response to the tumultuous history of South Africa through which she lived much of the remainder of her life.

3

A Returned South African

Schreiner returned to South Africa in October 1889 and, apart from brief visits to England in 1893 and 1897, she lived in the country of her birth until the end of 1913 when she travelled to Europe, seeking treatment for her heart condition. She was in England during the First World War, returning to South Africa in 1920, where she died, aged 65. South Africa fascinated her, and at the beginning of the 1890s she began to write essays on the country, its people and politics. These were explicitly conceived as the thoughts of a 'returned' South African, seeing her country anew, and seeking to understand and theorize the interdependence of its racial and ethnic groups. A new phase in Schreiner's life had begun, and her writing practices partially changed as a result. As well as a series of long essays on Boer life and South African history, many of her important publications over the next twenty years responded to specific and urgent events such as the Anglo-Boer war of 1899–1902, or the legislation which unified the separate states of South Africa in May 1910. Responding to the tumultuous course of South African's history called for new types of writing which fused polemic, journalism and literary practice. Through her political allegiances and activities, her probing, exhortatory letters, her relations with family and friends and in her polemical writing and her fiction, Schreiner sought to pinpoint, analyse and contest the structural inequalities which modernization entrenched. Her writing became a form of hand-to-hand combat with daily events.

In later twentieth-century apartheid South Africa Schreiner was attacked for being, in the words of the novelist Nadine Gordimer, 'the broken-winged albatross of white liberal thinking'.[1] Anti-apartheid politics of that period were dominated by a

Marxist analysis that generally condemned liberalism. However, more recently, liberal ideas have begun to be reassessed and, in turn, Schreiner's rhetorical strategies and forms of analysis have been re-examined and more generously judged. It is clear to see in her writing that she became increasingly conscious of how the colonial context of South Africa produced distinctive effects in relation to issues which had been important throughout the 1880s – issues of gender, class, political power and labour. In South Africa, these ideas had to be reassessed, as she intimated in one of her essays on South Africa: 'An intention, which leaves Europe a white-garbed bird of peace and justice, too often turns up, after six thousand miles' passage across the ocean, a black-winged harbinger of war and death' (*TSA* 204–5). Class politics in South Africa were necessarily enmeshed with race and, by the mid-1890s, Schreiner argued for a reformed middle class able to represent the interests of labouring natives against aggressive discriminatory policies being pursued by the government of the Cape Colony, headed by Cecil Rhodes. As tensions grew between South Africa's white populations, she supported the Boers against the British, believing them to be the only group able to resist the alliance of British imperialism and capitalism she saw as threatening South Africa's future.

By 1908, responding to the process of drafting the country's new constitution, Schreiner's allegiances again substantially shifted. Her anti-imperial, pro-Boer stance was superseded as the former white antagonists, Boer and British, allied to secure and entrench white supremacy. Even as she wrote and argued for the Boer cause in the 1890s, she had been presciently aware that the British–Boer controversy was transient, insisting to the Cape politician John X. Merriman that 'There are two and only two questions in South Africa, the native question and the question – Shall the whole land fall into the hands of a knot of Capitalists' (*OSL* 278). In 1898, she was trying to find out more about Toussaint L'Ouverture, wondering if an article about a black 'great man of genius' in a colonial newspaper might be a powerful means of countering essentialist notions of racial difference.[2] Writing in 1908 in the context of discussion about South Africa's future political structure, she warned that racism would be the defining problem of the twentieth century. Vociferously opposed to the 1913 Natives Land Act (which created land reserves for black Africans and barred them from purchasing land held by whites), she turned much of her energy to the cause of African labour and civil rights, often with a keen focus on how women were affected by racist legislative measures such as the pass laws which limited Africans' movement.

In 1980, Gordimer was scathing about Schreiner's feminism, deeming it an irrelevance in the face of South Africa's historical situation.[3] As this chapter shows, however, the connectedness of forms of social oppression is a central feature of Schreiner's analysis and her literary imagination. It accounts for the complexity of her colonial politics – both their limitations and their socially transformative potential. Schreiner publicly resigned in 1909 from the Cape Women's Enfranchisement League (which she helped to set up, attending meetings from 1907 and becoming vice-president) when it adopted a franchise policy which excluded non-white women. She wrote over a suffrage leaflet: 'the women of the Cape Colony *all* the women of the Cape Colony. These were the terms on which I joined' (*OSB* 262–3). The position of women, to which she devoted so much of her thinking and writing in the 1880s, was central to how she conceived of the wider politics of social justice in her country of birth but, in turn, must be brought into direct dialogue with those politics.

GREED AND EMPIRE: *THE POLITICAL SITUATION* AND *THOUGHTS ON SOUTH AFRICA*

Schreiner arrived back in South Africa as both a literary celebrity and a member of a family with growing influence and connections in the Colony. Her brother Will became a Member of Parliament, serving in 1893 as Attorney General in Rhodes's second ministry and, in 1898, as Prime Minister. Reputation and connections helped her gain access to the most influential players in Cape politics and, over the next decades, to a wide constituency of powerful figures in South Africa. She became friends with Jessie Innes and Mary Sauer whose husbands, James Rose Innes and J. W. Sauer, were amongst her correspondents. They, like John X. Merriman, another frequent correspondent, were important Cape politicians. Isie Smuts, whose husband Jan Smuts became the Transvaal's State Attorney and fought on the Boer side during the war, was also a friend, and Schreiner corresponded frequently with both.[4] Though there were often arguments and disagreements – Merriman was fiercely opposed to women entering public life, for instance – Schreiner influenced a wide range of public figures, using her letters to gather information, lobby and cajole. In March 1890, she moved from Cape Town to Matjesfontein, a small settlement on the railway line north of Cape Town. There she met for the first time the already legendary Cecil John Rhodes.

An admirer of *The Story of an African Farm*, Rhodes was an immensely powerful figure in the Colony's politics when Schreiner returned, having become enormously wealthy as a mining magnate at the Colony's Diamond Fields under the auspices of his company, De Beers. He was also a member of parliament and Schreiner was initially enthusiastic, calling him 'the only big man we have here'. There were even rumours of a romantic liaison between them. Nevertheless, she worried about him becoming Prime Minister of the Cape in 1890, believing that the role would conflict with the activities of his British South Africa Company. The Company had been granted a royal charter in 1889 to colonize Mashonaland and Matabeleland with a view to developing their mineral wealth. This area of southern Africa was named Rhodesia in 1895 and is now Zimbabwe (*OSL* 175). Though it was considered by members of the Colony's white elite a 'social coup' to have both Rhodes and (the now famous) Schreiner to dine at the same time, Schreiner was soon clear that their political differences precluded friendship (*OSB* 199). Already dismayed by his support in 1890 and 1891 for the Masters and Servants Act Amendment Bill, which permitted whites to beat their black servants, and suspicious of the increasing control he had of the Colony's press, by 1892 she was actively insisting that she did not want her name associated with his in any way (*LiOS* 213).[5] When she moved to Kimberley in July 1894, Schreiner was shocked by the property, power and influence of the 'monopolists' who dominated the diamond industry, foremost amongst which was the now immensely powerful De Beers Consolidated Company.

The consensus amongst English-identified liberals in Cape politics at this point identified the 'retrogressive' force as the Boers. The Boers were commonly seen as backward-looking, and unabashedly discriminatory in relation to the black African population. But Schreiner soon concluded that the greatest danger to the future of South Africa lay not with the supposedly 'anti-progressive' Boers, but rather in the alliance between imperialism and capitalism so powerfully embodied by Rhodes. She saw Boer racism as belonging to an old world, the result of prejudice which would inevitably transform as wider social change took hold. By contrast, Rhodes represented a systemic, dangerous new phenomenon of modern monopolistic capitalism working to service the interests of powerful individuals, decoupled from all progressive ideals or respect for national boundaries. Rhodes was personally ruthless – capable, Schreiner believed, of corruption and illegality in his politics – and driven by values which gave the lie to high-flown imperialist rhetoric. Schreiner was horrified to hear Rhodes say 'I prefer land to niggers' – a phrase she publicly attributed to him in her allegory story, *Trooper Peter Halket of Mashonaland* (*LiOS* 215). She believed he manipulated the racist and retrogressive propensities of the Cape Boers, 'by throwing the native to them to be torn to pieces' (*OSL* 278). Nevertheless, she also knew that 'If Rhodes were to die tomorrow, we should be free of the most energetic of the capitalists, but capitalism would be with us still' (*OSL* 326). Much later, on the eve of the political unification of South Africa in 1910, an act which entrenched white power, she wrote to the once-liberal Boer politician, F. S. Malan, of the alliances being struck between former white antagonists: 'It is not love that is uniting you all – it is greed. Cheap land, cheap labour, cheap mines, exploit the nigger – *that* is the bond that is uniting you!'[6] But in the 1890s, Schreiner still hoped that the Boers could function as a political force powerful enough to counter the corrosive effects of the country's wealthy capitalist elite.

Turning to colonial politics had significant ramifications for Schreiner's personal life too. In 1892 she read and admired a leader in a Cape newspaper attacking Rhodes; shortly after this, staying with friends in the Cradock district, its author, a young farmer called Samuel Cron Cronwright, rode over to meet her from his neighbouring farm. After a period of indecision the two

67

married in February 1894, with Cronwright agreeing to take his famous wife's name. The wish to have a child played a significant part in Schreiner's decision and, in April 1895, she gave birth to a daughter. 'Such a great, beautiful strong creature', she later wrote to her friends Dr and Mrs Brown. The baby, however, lived for only a few hours, and a grief-stricken Schreiner held its body for ten hours afterwards (*OSB* 214–15). In subsequent years she suffered the bitter disappointment of perhaps four or five miscarriages, and wrote sadly in 1899 to Havelock Ellis of not being a mother to children, 'creating them and feeling their dear soft hands on me' (*MOS* 477).

In part to recover from her baby's death – its small coffin was moved from place to place as Schreiner moved, and the child was eventually buried with its mother – and in part perhaps as a result of Cronwright's encouragement, Schreiner began to use her writing more directly to influence events in South Africa. In 1895, she and Cronwright co-authored a pamphlet on *The Political Situation*. It attacked Rhodes and the 'small band of Monopolists' controlling Cape politics (*PS* 18). She promised to send copies to friends in England, playfully writing to Edward Carpenter: 'It's really too bad you English sending out your bloated millionaires to eat us up! And the English people backing it and calling it "extending the Empire"!' (*OSL* 258). Her critical views on Britain and empire were hardening and she would soon describe imperialism as 'the euphonious title of a deadly disease'.[7]

The Political Situation warns against the destructive effects of capitalism in a culture where political traditions were highly individualistic and, most crucially, where class and labour issues were complicated by race. Schreiner believed that monopolistic capitalists – emblematized by Rhodes – were able to make enormous wealth which then funded access to political power. This power in turn facilitated greater economic exploitation and personal gain. South Africa was transformed in Schreiner's rhetoric into a test case of modernity: capitalism was not necessarily productive of even the partial forms of social and political advance experienced in Britain – she wrote to W. T. Stead of South Africa 'rolling back back back!' (*OSL* 256). Countering an increasingly active imperial propaganda which racialized and displaced anxieties about decline onto the colonial population of Boers, Schreiner sought to redefine 'backwardness' as an ethical (rather than ethnic) quality. Cape governance under Rhodes became markedly less liberal during the 1890s, with aggressive legislative measures that extended white control of African labour. The 1892 Franchise and Ballot Act raised the property franchise, in the process disqualifying most of the Cape's non-white voters. In one of her essays about South Africa, Schreiner described 'the relation between the foreign Speculator, Capitalist, and Shareholding class, and the black labouring class...[as] the very core within the core, and the kernel within the kernel, of the South African problem' (*TSA* 273).

In *The Political Situation* she and Cronwright sketched out strategies of resistance in relation to key policy areas of taxation, the franchise and, most urgently, labour. Schreiner argued that a progressive political collectivity must be forged, based on a reformed middle class.[8] Though she had been fiercely critical of the middle classes during the 1880s, this new South African middle class, emerging as it was in a period of crisis, must be ethically fit to combat voracious capitalist power and to protect and represent the excluded African population. She lamented to Edward Carpenter that such a middle class as yet barely existed: 'There are money-making whites, and down-trodden blacks, and nothing between' (*OSL* 215). The creation of this class was also a feature of Schreiner's essays about Boer life and culture. These essays, first appearing in journals and newspapers through the 1890s, were published posthumously as *Thoughts on South Africa* (1923). In them, Schreiner attempted to define a common culture which would spearhead the future 'blended South African Nation' (*TSA* 215). John Kucich has shown how this vision of a future melding of South Africa's white population was rooted for Schreiner in a still-potent evangelical culture: evangelical values of martyrdom, self-denial and love of freedom, she argued, were equally held by 'The Englishman' (the title of one of Schreiner's essays) and the Boer, and would provide the psychological and moral ground for their amalgamation.

Schreiner was attempting to present values and virtues of the Dutch-descended farming community as recognizable and familiar to her English audience. In doing so, however, she alienated parts of the Afrikaner population which was increasingly urban and educated, and hostile to being represented in the British press as uncivilized agrarians (*OSL* 274). Evoking the connective power of evangelical values was in any case, as Kucich concludes, a mistake. Evangelicalism had largely relocated to the lower-middle class in Britain, a class hostile to Schreiner's anti-imperialist and anti-war stance.[9] Although after the war Schreiner focused more attention on the prospect of an emerging black middle class – potentially a more successful constituency for her arguments about social equality – in the 1890s she strategically (and, perhaps, emotionally) backed the Boers in her effort to 'interpret South Africa to Britain'.[10]

'IF CHRIST CAME TO SOUTH AFRICA': *TROOPER PETER HALKET OF MASHONALAND*

The Political Situation was delivered by Cronwright to a meeting of the Kimberley English Farmer's Association in August 1895. In the short space of time before it appeared as a print pamphlet in 1896, Rhodes was in serious trouble. This was the result of a botched plan to seize control of the neighbouring Transvaal region. Ten years earlier, rich gold reserves had been discovered in the Boer Republic of the Transvaal, and Rhodes saw an opportunity to use complaints about the rights and privileges of the 'Uitlanders' – the European 'outsiders' or non-Boers drawn to the gold diggings at Johannesburg – as an excuse to wrest control of the area from the Boer government. Rhodes already had personal capital invested in Transvaal gold and he saw the Boer Republics as an obstacle to speedy industrialization and profit-making, and to British influence more generally. The attempted coup, known as the Jameson Raid, after Dr L. S. Jameson, Rhodes' subordinate who led Chartered Company troops into the Transvaal, spectacularly failed and Rhodes was forced to resign as the Cape's Prime Minister. Cape politics were rocked to the core. New divisions emerged with sharpened opposition between pro-Rhodes advocates of British intervention and their opponents (including Schreiner) who were now explicitly and overtly sympathetic to the Transvaal and the Boer cause. These new alignments crystallized the tensions which, by the decade's end, erupted in the 1899 Anglo-Boer war.

Schreiner was initially elated, believing that Rhodes could not recover, and writing to her friend (and Rhodes' supporter) W. T. Stead that 'the clouds have broken' (*OSL* 262). But other and unexpected consequences were soon claiming her attention. The diversion of South African Chartered Company forces (which were effectively Rhodes' private army) to the Transvaal, had opened an opportunity for African resistance to the Company's activity in the area north of the Limpopo river which in 1895 was renamed 'Rhodesia'. The Ndebele and Shona peoples of this region, historically antagonists, combined in the *Chimurenga* or war of liberation of 1896–7. Company reprisals were swift and savage. Schreiner was horrified by the violent response to what she viewed as legitimate political rebellion: 'The way they are hounding the Mashonas for what they call *murders* – i.e. for killing people in time of war – is to me far more terrible than anything that is happening in the Colony.... The English people are given up to their lust for gold and Empire and there is nothing left to appeal to' (*OSL* 287).[11]

Schreiner's distress was compounded by the fact that her mother, and her brother and sister, Theo and Ettie, were vehemently pro-Rhodes. Family tensions were consequently acute. Depressed and unwell, Schreiner went in the summer of 1896 for a break at the seaside where, 'as I woke, and as I opened my eyes there was an allegory full fledged in my mind! A sort of allegory story about Matabeleland' (*OSL* 288). This novella-length story, *Trooper Peter Halket of Mashonaland*, was conceived as a pragmatic political intervention, and indicted Rhodes by name, appealing directly to the English population with the ultimate aim of revoking the South Africa Company's Charter. Schreiner travelled to England early in 1897 to oversee its publication, ironically sharing the passage with Rhodes and his cohorts who were en route to appear before a Parliamentary Committee of Enquiry into the Jameson Raid. The book appeared to mixed reviews, few of which engaged seriously with its political themes. Some were repelled by the fictional device at the story's heart – the image of 'Lord Jesus Christ discussing South African politics', as one commentator put it.[12] Schreiner later acknowledged it was 'a dead failure' as a political pamphlet, not forcing a parliamentary enquiry into what was happening in Rhodesia or saving one African life. She nevertheless had not 'for one moment regretted' publishing it, and was glad that she did not let herself be bullied by warnings that Rhodes would sue her (*OSL* 333).

Trooper Peter Halket of Mashonaland features, within an apparently realist narrative, the appearance – in a manner one reviewer deemed 'little less than blasphemy' – of the 'extraordinary Interlocutor', Jesus Christ.[13] The bare plot of the novella is simple: Peter Halket is a young, working-class Englishman come to South Africa to make his fortune. After a period working at the Cape's diamond mines, he signs up as a mercenary for Rhodes' Chartered Company which is engaged in quelling the Matabele resistance. Accidentally separated from his troop, he has to spend a night alone on the veldt and is there joined by an unnamed figure whom readers (and, eventually, Peter) recognize as Christ. Through the night the stranger talks of exploitation, cruelty and human love, and indicts the actions of Rhodes. His soliloquy is part Socratic questioning and part Sermon on the Mount. It evokes a prospect of human evolution modified and directed by self-conscious ethical agency. He then calls on Peter Halket, in the fashion of evangelical missionaries, to take his message to those who need to hear it – to the English, to South Africans or even to just one other person (*TPH* 80–3). Peter protests his unpreparedness for such a task. However, the following day he returns to his troop where he pleads for the release of a recently captured African. Ordered instead to guard him, and then execute him the following day, Peter frees the prisoner and is himself shot dead by the troop's captain.[14]

Much of the force of *Trooper Peter* lies in its dense weave of symbols, and how their interactions dramatize the urgency of making the connections that constitute ethical truthfulness.[15] At the beginning of the story, alone in the vast darkness of the African veldt, Peter fantasizes about becoming rich in South Africa, like Rhodes. His confused thought processes highlight the incompatibility of free enterprise individualism – 'All men made money when they came to South Africa – Barney Barnato, Rhodes... why should not he!' (*TPH* 32) – and the monopoly conditions of the British South Africa Company. Peter's attempt to imagine a great 'Gold Mining Company' of his own flounders and fails because he cannot 'calculate' properly. In other words, Schreiner uses Peter's naivety about financial speculation to reveal the operations of instrumental reason: he cannot fix on calculating gain but becomes side-tracked by thinking of human costs (what of those who fail to sell their shares at the right time?).[16] In other words, Peter unwittingly stumbles upon Marx's famous dictum that market relations harm human relations.

Schreiner exploits the gap between what Peter consciously thinks and knows and what seeps out, unconsciously and unbidden, when he is alone on the veldt. Seated by his fire feeling hungry and lonely, Peter's avaricious fantasies about South Africa merge with memories of his rural English upbringing, overseen by his loving but impoverished washer-woman mother. Eventually, his thoughts become 'a chain of disconnected pictures' (*TPH* 35). These give a different vision of his South African life, horrifically reordering his childhood memories, and pointing to the human costs of the dream of Africa's wealth and plenty:

> Now, as he looked into the crackling blaze, it seemed to be one of the fires they had made to burn the natives' grain by, and they were throwing in all they could not carry away: then, he seemed to see his mother's fat ducks waddling down the little path with the green grass on each side.... Then – he saw the skull of an old Mashona blown off at the top, the hands still moving. He heard the loud cry of the native women and children as they turned the maxims on to the kraal....Then again he was working a maxim gun, but it seemed to him it was more like the reaping machine he used to work in England, and that what was going down before it was not yellow corn, but black men's heads; and he thought when he looked back they lay behind him in rows, like the corn in sheaves. (*TPH* 36)

This horrific phantasmagoria, which turns food production into mass killing, starkly ironizes the images of rural England retrieved in Peter's memory. Idealized English pastoral whole-someness, symbolized by the threshing machine, is transformed into mechanized slaughter and its bitter harvest is counted in lives despatched by the modern maxim gun. The ordinariness of agrarian life is common to Peter and the black Africans he has killed, a connection he will be forced to make as he comes to recognize their common humanity.

Descriptions of food – rice and mealies – plundered or destroyed on the one hand, or lovingly given to others on the other, occur again and again in the novella. In the second part of the book, set at the troop's camp, the men keep fires burning throughout the heat of the day where their pots cook these same staples. Provisions are all but exhausted; the men are hungry, and only their despised Captain eats well. Peter loses the rest of his troop as they transport (stolen) mealies and rice to the next camp. Glimpsing nothing on the veldt except the evidence of 'a down-trampled and now uncultivated mealie field', he is soon very hungry himself (*TPH* 26). But it is his spiritual emptiness that begins to be modified when the stranger appears and tells Peter of his own 'forty days and nights' hungering in the wilderness. Peter at last begins to understand that it is possible to be in South Africa for something other than making money: 'If you don't want to make money, what did you come to this land for? No one comes here for anything else', is his initial puzzled question (*TPH* 60). Food marks hierarchy – the troopers resent their Captain's access to superior food stuffs – and power. But in opposition to the destroyed native settlements, with burned granaries and trampled mealie fields, food is also emblematic of love, the source of the human ethic the story advocates. The stranger tells Peter of an old black woman who gives corn to her young companion in an effort to save the younger one's life even though it means the old woman's own death, and Peter Halket wraps mealies and rice in his handkerchief for the African prisoner he releases (*TPH* 49–50, 114). Throughout, the dense web of biblical reference and metaphor gradually accumulates and intensifies themes of spiritual hunger and material greed until Peter's own spiritual starvation ends with his last uneaten supper, which he saves to give to the African prisoner. This man, Peter has eventually understood, is hungry too, and Peter's act connects the gaps and disconnections which form the underside of his ambition to get rich quickly at the expense of others.

Peter has killed and looted, and he has also raped and abused black women, acts he tries to hide in his mind from memories of his mother. He and another trooper encounter and rape a young woman – 'her baby on her back, but young and pretty... and a black woman wasn't white!' (*TPH* 37). As the stranger talks,

Peter realizes that she is the same young woman whose life the old African woman attempts to protect at the cost of her own. The old woman, the stranger tells Peter, will die of starvation that very night (*TPH* 62). Peter's hallucinatory and fragmented images of Africa are forced into a different kind of focus, which Schreiner aims to make her readers see too. The rape of the black woman is also connected to Peter's initially bragging account of the African women who lived with him when he worked as a private prospector. These women, purchased and used for sex and domestic and agricultural labour, signal that the violence and malaise of the colonial enterprise is not confined to war and conflict: it is endemic in the culture.[17]

Schreiner told her brother, Will, that *Trooper Peter* was aimed at 'the great British public' (*OSL* 299). In the long section where the stranger recounts the story of a 'little preacher' rejected by his flock for speaking out against Rhodes, the narrative explicitly discusses the need to make connections (the preacher's congregation enjoys a biblical tale about the inalienable right to one's land, but are furious when he reads from the Cape parliament's report on the violent colonizing land grabs of the British South Africa Company). The passage is also as centrally about rhetoric and persuasion, however. The questions the stranger puts to Peter are rhetorical – 'What is a Christian? ... here, in this world, what is a Christian?' (*TPH* 59). But they are not merely rhetorical, Schreiner intimates: these are the real and urgent questions that she directs at 'the great British public'.

The first edition of *Trooper Peter* included a photographic frontispiece.[18] It shows three African men, hanged from a tree. Behind them, in a semi-circle, and gazing out to meet the viewer's answering look, are a group of white men who have, presumably, undertaken this chilling execution. It is a shocking image, meant to unsettle (it was removed from all subsequent editions and only restored in 1974). In the narrative Peter refers to this hanging 'spree', and the stranger tells him that he was with the men when they died. Peter's response – that he had seen the photograph of 'our fellows' but 'I didn't see you in it' (*TPH* 51) – intensifies the effect of Schreiner's weaving of documented event into her allegoric tale. The hanging tree of the frontispiece becomes another of the story's repeated motifs. It binds together the picture of the crucified Christ with outstretched arms that hangs in the schoolroom of Peter's remembered childhood, and the tree at the camp which dominates the second half of the book. Stunted and bleached white, its misshapen branches outspread like arms, it is this tree to which the African prisoner is tied so closely that 'they seemed one' (*TPH* 117). Blood has flowed from the man's bound feet, just as the blood drips in the schoolroom image of the crucified Christ. The narrative is both centripetal and centrifugal: images continually wind back, gathering further associations that point to the gulf between (Christian) ethical value and colonial plunder. On the veldt, Peter notices wounds in the stranger's feet and comments: 'You've been in the wars, too, I see', thus linking the crucifixion imagery with war and serving to set off another series of contrasts between the stranger's own wars against oppression, misery and cruelty and the colonial wars orchestrated by Rhodes; and between Christ's Company which values human bonds and the Chartered Company's materialism and greed (*TPH* 48).

In *Trooper Peter* Schreiner sought to shrink the safe distance maintained by British metropolitan readers from the raw violence of expansionist policy and practice in South Africa. Settler colonialism and imperial-backed expansionism are alike violent and exploitative processes, as Peter's inadvertent linking of his abuse of black women before and during the war demonstrates. At the book's end, another (unnamed) English trooper concludes, 'There is no God in Mashonaland' (*TPH* 121). In making Christ come to the South African veldt, Schreiner sought to unsettle those who identified themselves with the modernity of God's absence as much as those who believed in Christ's message. All were failing to make appropriate connections in implicitly sanctioning imperial activity in South Africa.

'THIS HELLISH WAR': *AN ENGLISH SOUTH AFRICAN'S VIEW OF THE SITUATION* AND 'EIGHTEEN-NINETY-NINE'

During the period immediately before the outbreak of war between Britain and the Boer Republics in October 1899, Schreiner was living in Johannesburg. The city, situated in the Boer Republic of the Transvaal, was the focus of the coming conflict. It had begun as a mining camp of 3,000 diggers following the discovery in 1886 of 'the most remarkable gold resource on earth' on the Witwatersrand.[19] A decade later, in the mid-1890s, it was a city of 100,000. Gold literally transfigured the place: the deep mining required an industrialized workforce and the policies used to create it were often dehumanizing and brutal. Capital poured into the area, together with an influx of stake-claimers, speculators, amalgamators and all the associated paraphernalia of a gold rush. Traditional native communities were uprooted, African labour was imported from elsewhere on the continent, and a disparate fortune-hunting European population streamed in, profoundly unsettling the area's agrarian structures and destabilizing the Transvaal government. Industrial modernization was experienced as a violent event: its processes were shockingly condensed and speeded up. Schreiner headed her letters from there 'Hell' or 'The City of Dreadful Night' (*OSL* 377, 366).

Johannesburg's 'Uitlanders' – the 'outsiders' or non-Afrikaners based in and around the mining industry and largely composed of British citizens – were the ostensible cause of conflict between the British government and the Boer Republic. Although the Jameson Raid had been embarrassing, Britain continued to protest that the Uitlanders were being treated unfairly in being denied citizenship rights by the Transvaal government. Some observers believed that foreign migrants were on the verge of outnumbering Afrikaners in the Transvaal and could be used to effect a change of power without the costs of war. This would secure Britain's long-term aim of a unified South Africa dominated by British business interests and British political practice.[20] However, this aim was overtaken by a more urgent sense that the Transvaal's vast mineral wealth must be promptly secured by the British – by war if necessary.

An active anti-war lobby in Britain opposed the conflict. Some were explicitly 'pro-Boer', while others were critical of a war forced on independent states for motives no higher than greed. One important figure in this respect was the reforming liberal theorist and commentator, J. A. Hobson. Hobson was recruited by the *Manchester Guardian* to cover the war, and his analysis both drew from and helped to consolidate Schreiner's own (he interviewed Schreiner for a book on the war). Like Schreiner, he believed that the war was orchestrated by a potent and dangerous new group of rapacious international capitalists, acting in concert and manipulating national interests for their own material gain. His thesis was elaborated in *Imperialism: A Study* (1902) which strongly influenced Lenin and helped shape Marxist thinking about the links between capitalism, imperialism and militarism. Hobson recruited Cronwright to tour England during the first half of 1900. Cronwright spoke at anti-war rallies and events, attacking the 'monopolists', defining the conflict as a 'capitalists' war', and tried to counter arguments about Boer racism and ill-treatment of black Africans. But national enthusiasm for the imperial cause intensified in 1900, culminating in the mass euphoria and street celebrations of 18 May 1900, when news of the relief of the besieged Mafeking reached London.[21] Cronwright had a difficult time as meetings were disrupted, describing on one occasion being 'mobbed... assaulted, mauled, and nearly killed' (*OALH* 67).

In South Africa, Schreiner was vilified in the British-supporting press, where she was lampooned as 'Olive Shrieker' (*OALH* 71). Tensions with family and friends also intensified. Her mother remained fervently pro-Britain, while her brother, Theo, was an active founding member of the South African Conciliation Committee, set up to support imperial policy and to counter pro-Boer propaganda. It was undoubtedly a difficult time. Schreiner spent part of the war years in Hanover, a town in the Cape. Martial law was in operation, and Schreiner was confined, as a pro-Boer, under a form of house arrest. She wrote of her isolation, of the problem of rising food prices and of receiving 'threatening letters and insulting cards' (*LiOS* 324). She ceaselessly lobbied against the war in the months preceding the outbreak of conflict, writing letters to her brother Will (then Prime Minister of the Cape), to Jan Smuts, who was State Attorney of the Transvaal Republic, and others. She cajoled and exhorted, exerting influence where she could. She sent reports to the *Manchester Guardian*, she cabled the journalist W. T. Stead, and was asked by the *New York Journal* to act as their war correspondent (*OALH* 55–82). Her anti-war pamphlet, *An English South African's View of the Situation*, which appeared first in newspapers in June 1899, was a last ditch effort to influence Sir Alfred Milner, the Governor and High Commissioner of the

Cape. Schreiner sent a proof copy to Milner, hoping he would read it while on board the train taking him to a summit at Bloemfontein with Paul Kruger, the Transvaal President. But talks there broke down, with Kruger concluding: 'It is our country you want'.[22]

Schreiner opens her pamphlet by identifying a peculiarly important South African voice. It is that of the 'African-born Englishman' who loves England and South Africa, and is equally bound to both (*ESAV* 4). Like much of her polemic, this pamphlet is acutely aware of its audience, and seeks to manipulate rhetoric and emotion connected to English national feeling. Schreiner focuses on distinguishing the extra-national forces of global capitalism which were making South Africa a 'hunting ground, a field for extracting wealth' (*ESAV* 56), and an England whose history and identity was also dangerously at risk. The pamphlet makes use of maternal metaphors familiar from English historical and imperial writing. In doing so, Schreiner aimed to counter those readers who dismissed her as 'anti-British'. Joseph Chamberlain's speech of 1897, on 'The True Conception of Empire', for example, warned against a Britain overly interested in 'pecuniary advantage', which 'was not truly a mother at all, but appeared rather in the light of a grasping and absentee landlord'.[23] Thomas Babington Macaulay had used the metaphor of the 'step-mother' to define England's national responsibility to 'make men patriotic' by benevolent assimilation. As Catherine Hall argues, it was an effectively deployed 'telling familial metaphor'.[24] Schreiner's essay aims to rework it by deeming England 'step-mother to this South African people' (*ESAV* 15). She then goes on to exploit the folkloric and fairy-tale associations of the 'evil' stepmother as contrasted with the good 'real' mother. England must become a 'real' mother if it is not to risk appearing horrifically 'unnatural': 'Is any position possible that could make necessary that mother and daughter should rise up in one horrible embrace, and rend, if it be possible, each other's vitals?' (*ESAV* 76). Aligning her account of England's role in South Africa with a Macaulayean history of England as progressive and assimilative was a strategic gesture on the eve of war.

Schreiner's writing, as well as her physical movement, was restricted during the war. Her letters were overseen by censors, which meant that her habitual form of lobbying was curtailed, and her main source of emotional support compromised. She wrote a number of short allegories about the conflict but the most important fictional response was her short story, 'Eighteen-Ninety-Nine', which was published posthumously in *Stories, Dreams and Allegories* (1923). It is a fictionalized fragment of the tales of Boer life and history Schreiner recreates in *Thoughts on South Africa* and *An English South African's View of the Situation*. The narrative begins in the early 1880s, with a Boer woman of about 50 and a younger woman, alone on their farm in the Northern Transvaal. The older woman's life has spanned the great events that make up Afrikaner nationalist history and myth. The Great Trek, when Boer farmers moved from the British administered Cape to found the two Boer Republics, the Orange Free State and the Transvaal, is part of her early memory. The dangers of settler life, to which the girl loses her parents and, eventually, her husband and her three sons, underline a harsh pastoral mythology of a blood-earned land. Each death means 'a new root driven deep into the soil... binding them to it' (*SDA* 18). The woman's memories eventually return the story to the present where her daughter-in-law, the widow of her youngest son, is about to give birth to a child.

Despite its naturalistic tone, the story is densely symbolic. It is saturated with images of cultivation: seasons unfold, maize and pumpkins are planted, husbanded and harvested. The women's bodies also produce bounty, in the form of the boy born at the story's start who becomes the focus of the women's attention, care, hope and love. They plan for his education, saving what money they earn to send him to school. But the boy is captivated by his grandmother's stories of Boer struggle and British oppression and, when war breaks out in 1899, he goes off to fight and is killed. The main narrative ends with the two women rising, grief-stricken, to plant seeds for the next harvest, the old woman reminding her daughter-in-law that the war might go on for a long time, and that 'our burghers must have food' (*SDA* 54). In *The Story of an African Farm*, Schreiner established herself, according to J. M. Coetzee, as 'the great anti-pastoral writer in South Africa', by creating a farm which mimics the emptiness of colonial culture.[25] The South African writer and critic Stephen Gray sees *African Farm* as inaugurating in fiction a literal and

80

moral landscape which 'dries the vital juices out of its inhabitants, stunts them and – worst of all – disallows them from achieving man's most sacred desire, the desire to take root in the land and belong'.[26] In 'Eighteen-Ninety-Nine', by contrast, Schreiner reworks the pastoral myth she had previously demolished. The simplicity of the women's agrarian lives – both literally and in terms of an implied moral economy – is a vivid contrast to the industrialized world of the gold-producing Rand with its fly-by-night speculators and investors. In the South African pastoral proper, however, the land is husbanded by men. As Coetzee puts it, the 'earth becomes wife to the husband-man'.[27] In Schreiner's story, by contrast, the women work the land together with their African servants, and they refuse the advances of neighbouring men who visit as suitors for the young widow. It overturns genre expectations just as they seem to be consolidated.

Schreiner's careful manipulation of generic expectations allows her to situate her story in relation to one of the most contentious aspects of the war. This concerned the British use of 'concentration' camps and related scandals about the sexual abuse and rape of unprotected Boer women. These were the focus of a major propaganda battle in the final years of the conflict. By the end of 1900 the main battles of the Boer war had been fought and – after initial setbacks – won by the British. However, conflict continued in the form of the small, mobile Boer commandos who continued exacting costs on British troops in what was effectively a guerrilla phase of the war. The British responded by burning farms, a policy designed to break the commandos' informal support networks and to demoralize combatants. Thousands of displaced Afrikaner and African refugees, composed mostly of women and children, were moved to camps where poor diet and unsanitary conditions resulted in widespread disease and horrific mortality. These tactics were dramatically deemed 'methods of barbarism' by the Liberal party leader, Henry Campbell-Bannerman. In turn, Campbell-Bannerman's combustible slogan was seized upon and used by the journalist W. T. Stead in a sensational attack on the conduct of British troops.

Stead's pamphlet, *Methods of Barbarism*, accused British soldiers of sexually molesting and raping vulnerable Boer women (as well as other offences against the 1899 Hague Convention rules on international warfare, including proscriptions against looting).[28] Stead ignited an argument about the farm-burning and concentration camps which focused on sexuality and masculinity. Incensed by Stead's accusations, Arthur Conan Doyle countered with *The War in South Africa: Its Cause and Conduct* in which he argued that unprotected Boer women and children had to be gathered together and secured as they otherwise risked being left 'in the presence of a large Kaffir population'.[29] Pro-imperial propaganda had devoted much time to highlighting Boer racist attitudes towards, and ill-treatment of, black Africans, contrasting this with the relatively liberal and benevolent policies and views of the British. However, in the camps controversies, fears of a rapacious and uncontrolled African sexuality began to be highlighted as a threat against which a responsible and civilized nation (Britain) must protect even combatant womenfolk. Both Stead and Doyle, opposed as they were, manipulated the same ideas of masculinity, class and nation, invoking either medieval notions of chivalry or a romanticized 'primitive' manliness popularized in imperial adventure fiction. For both, women were passive recipients of either masculine predation or of protection, and their treatment was the test of British civilized behaviour.

In 'Eighteen-Ninety-Nine', Schreiner's women-focused farm implicitly challenges the gender stereotypes underlying this debate. It is crucial to the story's meaning that the women work the farm alone for eighteen years before the boy's death. The South African pastoral invariably makes African labour invisible but here the women's dependence on their African workers is explicit: the grandmother buries her husband with Africans' help, for instance, 'with no white men near' (*SDA* 18). They are imperilled, in other words, not because of a threatening African sexuality, or because they are unprotected by men, but because of British war policy. There are two brief postscripts to the story: the first, 'Nineteen Hundred and One', describes the unmarked graves of the two women who have both perished in a concentration camp from 'hunger and want' (*SDA* 56). The following postscript 'In the Year Nineteen Hundred and Four' confirms that the farm was torched by English soldiers, and that the domestic objects with which the story begins are now mementos in English homes. These objects include the grandmother's stool, on which the boy sat to hear her stories, and the flintlock gun which belonged to her husband and with which he shot the lion that killed him. The stool is now a curiosity in a London drawing-room, the woman gratified that her soldier son had thought of her 'while away in the back country' (*SDA* 57). The gun, which the widow hung on the wall and polished every day, now adorns the wall of a country house in England, and its new owner shows it off, proud of its age and value. War looting merges with the capitalist cash nexus to drain the objects of their original material and emotional value. Instead, their symbolism signals Schreiner's critique of the degraded culture and commercial values which had propelled Britain into war.

It is unclear whether Schreiner ever planned to publish 'Eighteen-Ninety-Nine'. There is abundant evidence that she continued to read fiction and poetry in the years following the war, often discussing her reactions in letters to friends. She also tried hard to complete *From Man to Man* during the first decade of the new century. But it is as if the experience of South Africa had developed a writing habit which responded to emergency. Schreiner continued to write and publish when spurred by political issues and causes, but her fiction-making seems to have become something done without a need for an audience, for her own fulfilment.

'THE WHOLE OLD WORLD IS CRACKING'

After the war, Schreiner's life remained difficult. Severed from the English-identified population of the Cape because of her war sympathies, she had little in common with the Boers about whom she became increasingly critical as the post-war settlement closed off progressive options. She was also treated with suspicion by black Africans because of her support for the Boer cause. In the decade following the conflict, she was often unwell and probably intermittently depressed. She lived apart from Cronwright much of the time and sometimes complained of isolation, writing to her brother at the end of 1908 from Matjesfontein in the Cape Colony where she lived for its clear air: 'I think what I need almost more than cool air is a little friendly intercourse.'[30] Nevertheless, she continued to engage in political issues, reading avidly and periodically supporting organized political activity. The position of women remained an important focus, especially in relation to political enfranchisement for women to which Schreiner hoped that *Woman and Labour* – which she was busy completing in 1909 – might contribute. Between 1905 and 1910 she was involved in campaigns about immigrant Chinese labour and Indian citizenship rights, highlighting the ill-treatment of imported labour but focused on the way such labour was used to weaken indigenous labour organization. She wrote an article condemning the persecution of Jews in 1906, and made an important written contribution to debate about the future of the South African constitution which appeared originally in the *Transvaal Leader*, and was reissued the following year as *Closer Union* (1909). In it, Schreiner anticipates the economic forces of globalization which would characterize the twentieth century, arguing that South Africa's 'great complex body of humanity' gave it a unique opportunity. It could either lead the way in forging a 'whole' humanity or else function as a bleak portent of the future. 'I would rather draw a veil over the future of this land', she warned, if Africans were dispossessed of land, exploited for labour, forced into urban environments in compounds and slums with their social organization broken (*CU* 50).

Within a few years, Schreiner had good reason to believe that the worst was already happening as the First World War began to exact its staggering human costs. Schreiner had travelled to Europe in 1913, seeking medical help for a now-serious heart condition. She was 58. Living in England at the outbreak of war, she remained there for its duration. By now she was a committed pacifist and this, combined with ill health and the antagonism and suspicion which greeted her German surname when she sought lodgings, made these difficult years. Although she remained in contact with a core group of close friends her opposition to the war damaged many old friendships. She admired and was in contact with prominent anti-war figures – Vernon Lee and Bertrand Russell amongst them (*LOS* 338) – but was disappointed in others. Mohandas Gandhi – who she admired and had sought out in South Africa, causing Gandhi to write: 'Fancy the author of *Dreams* paying a tribute to passive resistance' (*OSB* 304) – she believed compromised the principles of *satyagraha* (or non-violent resistance) by his support for the British in the conflict.[31] Between bouts of incapacitating illness, she wrote anti-war allegories and public letters on conscientious objection, as well as attending some of the tribunals set up to try conscientious objectors. Her most sustained literary writing was 'The Dawn of Civilisation', an unfinished piece on war and human aggression, an extract of which appeared posthumously in the *Nation and Athenaeum* in 1921.

After the war's end, in 1920, Schreiner returned to South Africa. Buoyed up for a while by the loving attention of family and friends, and the 'real bread, fresh fish', she could eat there after the restricted diet of the war years, she was soon very ill and began to talk about dying (*OSB* 324–5). She found it difficult to find lodgings and worried about taking money from her husband. Schreiner had thought a good deal about hope which she understood to be as central a feature of human emancipation as any material change. In 1908, she wrote to Cronwright about conversing with Keir Hardie about 'the joy, and hope, and passion of enthusiasm with which we worked' in the 1880s, insisting that 'it was not for nothing', and that real advances in the conditions of working-class life had been made (*OSL* 278). In 1914, she wrote far more sadly to Edward Carpenter of the war that was 'simply crushing us, who had such hopes for the future 20 years ago' (*OSL* 340), and to Emily Hobhouse of how military conflict on this scale 'draws out all that is basest in the human heart' (*OSL* 341). But back in South Africa, and near the end of her own life, she wrote to her lifelong friend Mary Brown of 'how slowly hope dies', acknowledging that 'it has been a wonderful beautiful thing for us to be alive' (*OSB* 322). Nor did her sense of what it means to engage in a swiftly-changing world, to recognize one's own limitations and yet to continue to think and argue and hope, ever diminish.

In her final months of life, Schreiner supported the defence of Samuel Masabalala, of the African National Congress, who helped organize a strike of African workers in Port Elizabeth and was in prison as a result. She collected money for African women imprisoned in Bloemfontein for opposing the introduction of the passes which controlled African labour (*OSB* 323). To

Jan Smuts, she wrote a few weeks before her death of her irritation on reading a speech by Edward, Prince of Wales, which celebrated Englishness and imperial ideals, insisting that the days of 'princes and bosses' were over: 'This is the 20th century; the past is past never to return, even in South Africa'.[32] Schreiner contributed to that process with her fervent embrace of new scientific and social ideas. Her restless intuition told her that literary convention must change in order to tell new stories, and she attempted to tell the story of modernization and progress – or more accurately to call it into being – through realist narrative, allegory, symbolic fiction, polemic, lecture, newspaper article, tract and in the thousands of letters she wrote. Her utopian hopes and visions were always made up, however, from elements of the human culture of her own life and experience – especially those connected to her religious upbringing and subsequent freethinking. Writing in 1892 to a minister who questioned her about faith, Schreiner acknowledged that her sense of a world made whole – gained by her as a young woman through a combination of romanticism, transcendentalism and evolutionary science – could be expressed in an 'older phraseology': 'There is NOTHING but God' (OSL 213; Schreiner's emphasis). Humans need ideals and dreams in order to be able to live.

In the last of the many boarding houses which were so often her temporary homes, Schreiner died of heart complications on the night of 10–11 December 1920, and was found the next morning by a maid who went in with her morning tea, propped up in bed with the book she had been reading open on her chest, wearing her reading glasses, with a pen in her right hand. She had left precise instructions about her final resting place, which was to be with her baby and favourite dog on the top of a mountain in the Karoo. Her reinterment happened the following year, when Cronwright returned to South Africa. In the meantime, she was temporarily buried in the Schreiner family plot in Cape Town. Cronwright's brother, Alfred, who presided over the burial, anxiously imposed his brother's instruction to allow no religious word to be said. So anxiously, indeed, that he allowed no word at all and 'perfect absolute silence' reigned. But when the small group of gathered family and friends turned in silence to leave, some of the women went back and laid palm leaves over the grave. The palms, Christian symbol of triumph, broke the imposed injunction at the same time as they filled the silence with a gesture of female love and mourning. Schreiner, who loved the power of symbols and who was never one to obey rules, would surely have approved.[33]

Notes

INTRODUCTION

1. *Saturday Review of Politics, Literature, Science and Arts*, 55 (21 April 1883), 507–8, 507.
2. There is disagreement about whether Schreiner was called Emily or Emilie: Liz Stanley asserts that the baptismal record shows 'Emily'; in a dairy entry, her husband Samuel Cron Cronwright-Schreiner explains that during the reinterment of her body at the top of Buffelskop, the mountain where she chose to be buried, the undertaker was instructed to correct the details on the coffin's name-plate from 'Emily Olive' to 'Olive Emilie Albertina'. Paul Walters and Jeremy Fogg (eds), *Olive Schreiner: her Reinterment on Buffelskop* (Grahamstown: National English Literary Museum, 2005), 106.
3. Schreiner decided almost immediately not to try to publish *Undine*, which appeared posthumously in 1929.
4. Yaffa Draznin, 'Did Victorian Medicine Crush Olive Schreiner's Creativity?', *Historian*, 47/2 (1985), 196–207.
5. All Schreiner's extant letters about publishing are helpfully collected together under 'Dealings with Editors and Publishers', Liz Stanley et al, *Olive Schreiner Letters Online* at http://www.olive schreiner.org/ [accessed 20 July 2012]. This site became available after this book was completed, although some of its material has been incorporated at revisions stage.
6. 'Review of *Dreams*', *Athenaeum*, 3298 (10 January 1891), 46–7.
7. *Athenaeum*, 4279 (17 December 1920), 829.
8. Winifred Holtby, 'Writers on South Africa', *The Bookman*, 76 (September 1929), 279–84, 280; Michael Harmel, 'Olive Schreiner – Fearless Fighter Against Injustice', *New Age* (10 March 1955).
9. Stanley et al, *Olive Schreiner Letters Online*.
10. Showalter famously lambasted Schreiner for her neurotic inability to write anything sustained, but later revised her own assessment. See Elaine Showalter, *A Literature of Their Own: British Women*

88

Novelists from Brontë to Lessing (London: Virago, 1978), 197 and 'Twenty Years On'. *A Literature of Their Own Revisited'*, *Novel. A Forum on Fiction*, 31/3 (Summer 1998), 399–413.
11. See entries in the Select Bibliography.
12. Havelock Ellis, *My Life* (London: Heinemann, 1940), 186.

CHAPTER 1: EVANGELICALISM, FREETHOUGHT AND LOVE: *UNDINE* AND *THE STORY OF AN AFRICAN FARM*

1. Henry Norman, 'Theories and Practice of Modern Fiction', *Fortnightly Review* 34 (December 1883), 870–86, 882.
2. Renier was the adopted child of Schreiner's close friend, Alice Corthorn.
3. Olive Renier, 'A South African Rebel', *The Listener* (7 April 1955), in Cherry Clayton (ed.), *Olive Schreiner* (Johannesburg: McGraw-Hill, 1983), 51–5, 53.
4. Charlotte Brontë, *Jane Eyre* (Oxford: Oxford University Press, 2000), 37.
5. A useful overview of Spencer is J. D. Y. Peel, *Herbert Spencer: The Evolution of a Sociologist* (London: Heinemann, 1971).
6. Canon McColl, 'An Agnostic Novel' and Edward Aveling, 'A Notable Book', in Clayton (ed.), *Olive Schreiner*, 72–3, 67–9.
7. John Stuart Mill, *Principles of Political Economy* ed. William J. Ashley (1909), Library of Economics and Liberty. http://www.econlib.org/library/Mill/mlP62.html [accessed 26 October 2012], IV, 7.8.
8. For readers interested in the biographical elements of *Undine*, these are discussed in *WSA;* Cherry Clayton, *Olive Schreiner* (New York: Twayne Publishers, 1997), 10–12, 29–39; Helen Bradford, 'Olive Schreiner's "Series of Abortions": Fact, Fiction and Teenage Abortion', *Journal of Southern African Studies*, 21/4 (1995), 623–41.
9. Laura Schwartz, 'Freethought, Free Love and Feminism: Secularist Debates on Marriage and Sexual Morality, England c. 1850–1885', *Women's History Review*, 19/5 (2010), 775–93.
10. W. T. Stead, 'The Book of the Month: the Novel of the Modern Woman', *Review of Reviews*, 10 (July 1894), 64–74, 64.
11. John Kucich, *Imperial Masochism: British Fiction, Fantasy, and Social Class* (Princeton and Oxford: Princeton University Press, 2007), 50.
12. Ibid. 94.
13. Ralph Waldo Emerson, 'Self-Reliance', in *Essays and Poems*, ed. Tony Tanner (London: Dent,1995), 23–46, 24.
14. Ralph Waldo Emerson, 'Napoleon, or the Man of the World', *Representative Men* (Leipzig: Tauchnitz, 1907), 220–56, 254.

15. For an extended reading of Gregory Rose, see Christopher Lane, *The Burdens of Intimacy: Psychoanalysis and Victorian Masculinity* (Chicago: University of Chicago Press, 1999), 93–118.
16. Elaine Showalter, *A Literature of Their Own: British Women Novelists from Brönte to Lessing* (London: Virago, 1978), 199.
17. Mordecai Tamarkin, *Cecil Rhodes and the Cape Afrikaners: The Imperial Colossus and the Colonial Parish Pump* (London & Portland: Frank Cass, 1996), 20–3.
18. Aveling, 'A Notable Book', 67.

CHAPTER 2: SEX WORK: *WOMAN AND LABOUR*, STORIES AND ALLEGORIES, *FROM MAN TO MAN*

1. Ruth Livesey, *Socialism, Sex, and the Culture of Aestheticism in Britain, 1880–1914* (Oxford: Oxford University Press, 2007), 78.
2. Kevin Manton, 'The Fellowship of the New Life: English Ethical Socialism Reconsidered', *History of Political Thought*, 24/2 (2003), 282–304.
3. A good overview of these debates can be found in Lucy Bland, *Banishing the Beast: English Feminism and Sexual Morality 1885–1914* (Harmondsworth: Penguin, 1995).
4. For full discussion of these ideas in relation to late nineteenth-century feminism, see Angelique Richardson, *Love and Eugenics: Rational Reproduction and the New Woman* (Oxford: Oxford University Press, 2003).
5. On the Contagious Diseases Acts, see Judith Walkowitz, *Prostitution and Victorian Society: Women, Class and the State* (Cambridge: Cambridge University Press, 1980). W. T. Stead, 'The Maiden Tribute of Modern Babylon', *Pall Mall Gazette* (6, 7, 8, 10 July 1885); see also Judith Walkowitz, *City of Dreadful Delight: Narratives of Sexual Danger in Late-Victorian London* (London: Virago, 1992).
6. Livesey, *Socialism, Sex, and the Culture of Aestheticism*, 18–43.
7. Quoted in Sheila Rowbotham, *Edward Carpenter: A Life of Liberty and Love* (London: Verso, 2008), 74.
8. Liz Stanley, *Imperialism, Labour and the New Woman: Olive Schreiner's Social Theory* (Durham: sociologypress, 2002), 81.
9. First and Scott in turn question Cronwright's account in *OSB*, 266–8.
10. Kate Flint, *The Woman Reader 1837–1914* (Oxford: Clarendon Press, 1993), 242.
11. Vera Brittain, *Testament of Youth* (1933; London: Weidenfeld & Nicolson, 2009), 24.
12. Sally Ledger, *The New Woman: Fiction and Feminism at the Fin de Siècle*

(Manchester: Manchester University Press, 1997), 43. See also Carol Barash, 'Virile Womanhood: Olive Schreiner's Narratives of a Master Race', in *Speaking of Gender*, ed. Elaine Showalter (London: Routledge, 1989), 269–81.

13. Morag Schiach notes that 25% of married women were employed in 1851, compared to 10% in 1911, in Morag Shiah, *Modernism, Labour and Selfhood in British Literature and Culture, 1890–1930* (Cambridge: Cambridge University Press, 2004), 5.

14. On Englishness and 'Teutonic virtues', see Peter Mandler, *The English National Character: The History of an Idea from Edmund Burke to Tony Blair* (New Haven: Yale University Press, 2005), 100–5.

15. Emma Francis, 'Olive Schreiner's *Woman and Labour*: God, Darwin and "the asthmatic Jew,"' paper given at the 18th and 19th Century British Women Writers Conference, University of Louisiana at Lafayette, 14–16th April 2005.

16. On the Men and Women's Club, see Walkowitz, *City of Dreadful Delight*, Bland, *Banishing the Beast*.

17. Pearson is discussed in Carolyn Burdett, *Olive Schreiner and the Progress of Feminism: Evolution, Gender, Empire* (Basingstoke: Palgrave, 2001), 49–77, and in Theodore M. Porter, *Karl Pearson: The Scientific Life in a Statistical Age* (Princeton and Oxford: Princeton University Press, 2004).

18. Greta Jones, *Social Darwinism and English Thought: the Interaction between Biological and Social Theory* (Sussex: Harvester, 1980), 54–77.

19. Karl Pearson, *National Life from the Standpoint of Science* (London: Black, 1901), 43–4.

20. See Richardson, *Love and Eugenics*.

21. Karl Pearson, quoted in Burdett, *Olive Schreiner and the Progress of Feminism*, 63.

22. See Shiach, *Modernism, Labour and Selfhood*.

23. Francis, 'Olive Schreiner's *Woman and Labour*'.

24. Livesey, *Socialism, Sex, and the Culture of Aestheticism*, 18–43, 15.

25. Olive Schreiner to T. Fisher Unwin, 14 February 1889, Harry Ransom Research Center, University of Texas at Austin, Olive Schreiner Letters Project transcription, lines 5-6, *Olive Schreiner Letters Online* at http://www.oliveschreiner.org/vre?view=collections&colid=22&letterid=11 [accessed 23 July 2012].

26. Livesey, *Socialism, Sex, and the Culture of Aestheticism*, 99.

27. H. G. Wells, in Sally Ledger and Roger Luckhurst (eds), *The Fin de Siècle: A Reader in Cultural History* (Oxford: Oxford University Press, 2000), 9.

28. William Greenslade, *Degeneration, Culture and the Novel: 1880–1940* (Cambridge: Cambridge University Press, 1994).

29. This analogy gave the title to William Booth's moral tract, *In Darkest*

England and the Way Out (1890). See Ledger and Luckhurst, *The Fin de Siècle*, 45–9.

30. See Paula M. Krebs, *Gender, Race, and the Writing of Empire: Public Discourse and the Boer War* (Cambridge: Cambridge University Press, 1999).
31. Stanley, *Imperialism*, 135.
32. Arthur Symons, Review of *Dreams*, *Athenaeum*, 3298 (10 January 1891), 46–7.
33. Ann Heilmann, *New Woman Strategies: Sarah Grand, Olive Schreiner, Mona Caird* (Manchester: Manchester University Press, 2004), 127.
34. Scott McCracken, 'Stages of Sand and Blood: the Performance of Gendered Subjectivity in Olive Schreiner's Colonial Allegories', in *Rereading Victorian Fiction* eds Alice Jenkins and Juliet John (Basingstoke: Palgrave, 2000), 145–58, 148.
35. Laura Chrisman, 'Allegory, Feminist Thought and the *Dreams* of Olive Schreiner', *Prose Studies: History, Theory, Criticism*, 13, 1 (May 1990), 126–150, 142.
36. McCracken, 'Stages of Sand and Blood', 153.
37. See Livesey, *Socialism, Sex, and the Culture of Aestheticism*, 84–5.
38. Olive Schreiner to Isaline Philpot, 26 March 1889, NLSA Cape Town, Special Collections, Olive Schreiner Letters Project transcription, lines 5–6, *Olive Schreiner Letters Online* at http://www.olives-chreiner. org/vre?view=collections&colid=137&letterid=345 [accessed 30 July 2012].
39. Havelock Ellis, 'Mescal: A New Artificial Paradise', *Contemporary Review*, 73 (Jan. 1898), 130–41, 131.
40. Laura Chrisman, 'Colonialism and Feminism in Olive Schreiner's 1890s Fiction', *English in Africa*, 20/1 (May 1993), 25–38, 31.
41. Constance Lytton and Jane Warton, *Prisons and Prisoners: Some Personal Experiences* (London: Heinemann, 1914), 159.
42. Quoted in Sally Ledger, *Henrik Ibsen* (Plymouth: Northcote House, 1999), 2.
43. Quoted ibid. 3.
44. See Rose Lovell-Smith, 'Science and Religion in the Feminist Fin-de-Siècle and a New Reading of Olive Schreiner's *From Man to Man*', *Victorian Literature and Culture*, 29/2 (2001), 303–26, 313.
45. Friedrich Engels, *The Origin of the Family, Private Property and the State* (1884; London: Penguin, 1986), 102.
46. Lovell-Smith, 'Science and Religion', 314.
47. Ibid. 319.
48. Charles Darwin, *The Descent of Man, and Selection in Relation to Sex* (London: Penguin, 2004), 689.
49. Carolyn Burdett, 'Sexual Selection, Automata and Ethics in George Eliot's *The Mill on the Floss* and Olive Schreiner's *Undine* and *From*

Man to Man', *Journal of Victorian Culture*, 14/1 (2009), 26–52, 45–6.
50. H. G. Wells, *The Time Machine* (1895; Harmondsworth: Penguin, 2005), 83.
51. Stanley, *Imperialism*, 96.
52. Ibid. 81.
53. Burdett, *Olive Schreiner and the Progress of Feminism*, 100.
54. Quoted in Stanley, *Imperialism*, 39.

CHAPTER 3: A RETURNED SOUTH AFRICAN

1. Nadine Gordimer, 'The Prison-House of Colonialism', in *An Olive Schreiner Reader: Writings of Women and South Africa*, ed. Carol Barash (London: Pandora, 1987), 221–7, 223.
2. Olive Schreiner to G.W. Cross, 21 April 1898, Cory Library, Olive Schreiner Letters Project transcription, lines 32–3. *Olive Schreiner Letters Online* at http://www.oliveschreiner.org/vre?view=collections &colid=8&letterid=15 [accessed 30 July 2012].
3. Gordimer, 'The Prison-House of Colonialism', 225–6.
4. Liz Stanley et al (eds), *Olive Schreiner Letters Online* contains the fullest information about Schreiner's correspondence: see http://www.oliveschreiner.org [accessed 30 July 2012].
5. Schreiner wrote a skit on Rhodes and his support for the Strop Bill in 1891, 'The Salvation of a Ministry', which is included in *LiOS*, 202–5.
6. Olive Schreiner to Francois Stephanus ('FS') Malan, 6 January 1909, National English Literary Museum, Grahamstown, Olive Schreiner Letters Project transcription, lines 113-15. *Olive Schreiner Letters Online* at http://www.oliveschreiner.org/vre?view=collections&colid =44&letterid=7 [accessed 30 July 2012].
7. In an essay on 'The South African Nation' (1900), included in *TSA*, 332–50, 341.
8. See John Kucich, *Imperial Masochism: British Fiction, Fantasy, and Social Class* (Princeton and Oxford: Princeton University Press, 2007), 107–24.
9. Ibid. 123.
10. This phrase forms a chapter heading of what is still one of the best accounts of this aspect of Schreiner's work: Paula M. Krebs, *Gender, Race, and the Writing of Empire: Public Discourse and the Boer War* (Cambridge: Cambridge University Press, 1999).
11. Now called Zimbabwe, the country's painful recent history, characterized by often violent 'land grabs', has chilling precedents in the actions of the Chartered Company.
12. Notice for *The Bookman* (March 1897), 182.

13. Anon., 'Recent Books: French and English', *Blackwood's Edinburgh Magazine*, 161 (April 1897), 455–84, 478.
14. Other than an excellent essay by the South African critic Stephen Gray, first published in 1975 (rpt. 'The Trooper at the Hanging Tree', in *Olive Schreiner* ed. Cherry Clayton (Johannesburg: McGraw Hill, 1983), 198–208), *Trooper Peter* has been generally overlooked until recently when it has been reassessed: see, for example, Laura Chrisman, *Rereading the Imperial Romance: British Imperialism and South African Resistance in Haggard, Schreiner, and Plaatje* (Oxford: Oxford University Press, 2000), 120–62; Liz Stanley, 'Encountering the Imperial and Colonial Past through Olive Schreiner's *Trooper Peter Halket of Mashonaland*', *Women's Writing*, 7/2 (2000), 197–219.
15. This theme of connections is developed in Burdett, *Olive Schreiner and the Progress of Feminism*, 124–35.
16. Chrisman, *Rereading the Imperial Romance*, 128.
17. See Chrisman, ibid. 141; and for a fuller reading of how these African women function in the narrative, Burdett, *Olive Schreiner and the Progress of Feminism*, 130–1.
18. For excavation of the background to the frontispiece, see Paul Walters and Jeremy Fogg, 'The Short Sorry Tale of *Trooper Peter Halket of Mashonaland* and its Frontispiece', *English Studies in Africa*, 53/2 (2010), 86–101.
19. Terence McCarthy and Bruce Rubidge, *The Story of Earth and Life* (Cape Town: Struik, 2005), 106.
20. Denis Judd and Keith Surridge, *The Boer War* (London: John Murray, 2002).
21. See Krebs, *Gender, Race, and the Writing of Empire*.
22. Judd and Surridge, *The Boer War*, 47.
23. Joseph Chamberlain, 'The True Conception of Empire', in *The Fin de Siècle: A Reader in Cultural History c. 1880–1900*, eds. Sally Ledger and Roger Luckhurst (Oxford: Oxford University Press, 2000), 137–41, 138.
24. Catherine Hall, 'Macaulay's Nation', *Victorian Studies*, 51/3 (2009), 505–23, 514, 520.
25. J. M. Coetzee, *White Writing: On the Culture of Letters in South Africa* (New Haven: Yale University Press, 1988), 4.
26. Stephen Gray, *Southern African Literature: an Introduction* (Cape Town: David Philip, 1979), 7.
27. Coetzee, *White Writing*, 7.
28. W. T. Stead, *Methods of Barbarism. 'War is War' and 'War is Hell': the Case for Intervention* (London: Review of Reviews, 1901).
29. Arthur Conan Doyle, *The War in South Africa: Its Cause and Conduct* (Toronto: Morang, 1902), 81–2. This discussion draws from Burdett, *Olive Schreiner and the Progress of Feminism*, 162–71.

30. Olive Schreiner to William Philip ('Will') Schreiner, 30 December 1908, UCT Manuscripts & Archives, Olive Schreiner Letters Project transcription, lines 19–20. *Olive Schreiner Letters Online* at http://www.oliveschreiner.org/vre?view=collections&colid=100&letter-id=73 [accessed 30 July 2012].

31. Liz Stanley and Helen Dampier, "'I trust that our brief acquaintance may ripen into sincere friendship'": Networks Across the Race Divide in conceptualising Olive Schreiner's Letters 1890–1920', *Letters, Letterness and Epistolary Networks: a Working Paper Series of the Olive Schreiner Letters Project* (2010), http://www.oliveschreiner letters. ed.ac.uk/GiantRaceArticlePDF.pdf [accessed 20 September 2011]

32. Olive Schreiner to Jan Smuts, 19 October 1920, National Archives Repository, Pretoria, Olive Schreiner Letters Project transcription, lines 61–2, *Olive Schreiner Letters Online* at http://www.oliveschrei-ner.org/vre?view=collections&colid=70&letterid=122 [accessed 30 July 2012].

33. Paul Walters and Jeremy Fogg (eds), *Olive Schreiner: her Reinterment on Buffelskop* (Grahamstown: National English Literary Museum, 2005), 14.

Select Bibliography

WORKS BY OLIVE SCHREINER

The Story of an African Farm [1883] (Oxford and New York: Oxford University Press, 1992).
Dreams (2nd edn.; London: Unwin, 1891).
Dream Life and Real Life: A Little African Story (London: Unwin, 1893).
The Political Situation (London: Unwin, 1896).
Trooper Peter Halket of Mashonaland [1897] (Parklands: AD. Donker, 1992).
An English-South African's View of the Situation: Words in Season (London: Stodder & Houghton, 1899).
A Letter on the Jew (Cape Town: Liberman, 1906).
Closer Union (London: Fifield, 1909).
Woman and Labour [1911] (London: Virago, 1982).
'The Dawn of Civilization', *Nation and Athenaeum* (26 March 1921).
Thoughts on South Africa [1923] (Parklands: A.D. Donker, 1992).
Stories, Dreams and Allegories (London: Unwin, 1923).
From Man to Man [1926] (London: Virago, 1982).
Undine (New York and London: Harper, 1928).
An Olive Schreiner Reader ed. Carol Barash (London: Pandora, 1987).

LETTERS

Cronwright-Schreiner, S.C. (ed.), *The Letters of Olive Schreiner* (London: Unwin, 1924). Selectively weighted towards letters to Havelock Ellis and Cronwright, and often containing omissions and inaccuracies.
Draznin, Yaffa (ed.), *My Other Self: the Letters of Olive Schreiner and Havelock Ellis 1884–1920* (New York: Peter Lang, 1992). Contains full correspondence between Schreiner and Ellis held at the Harry Ransom Humanities Research Center, USA.
Rive, Richard (ed.), *Olive Schreiner Letters, vol I: 1871–1899* (Oxford: Oxford University Press, 1988). An important collection although

only containing letters to 1899, and with some problematic transcription.

Stanley, Liz et al, *Olive Schreiner Letters Online* at http://www.olives-chreiner.org/ [accessed 23 July 2012]. *OSLO* provides open access to nearly 5,000 of Schreiner's extant letters as fully searchable transcriptions from 2012. This is the most important publishing event for Schreiner scholarship in recent years.

BIOGRAPHIES

Cronwright-Schreiner, S. C., *The Life of Olive Schreiner* (London: Unwin, 1924). The original account of Schreiner's life on which other biographers have drawn. Although important, its assessment is filtered through Cronwright's self-serving and often distorting construction of her as a neurotic genius.

Ellis, Havelock, *My Life* (London: Heinemann, 1940). A significant section deals with Ellis's relationship with Schreiner.

First, Ruth and Ann Scott, *Olive Schreiner: A Biography* (London: Andre Deutsch, 1980). The best existing biography of Schreiner's whole life by a prominent anti-apartheid campaigner (First) and a British feminist (Scott).

Schoeman, Karel, *Olive Schreiner: A Woman in South Africa 1855–1881* (Johannesburg: Jonathan Ball, 1991). An invaluable portrait of South African missionary and colonial culture.

——, *Only an Anguish to Live Here: Olive Schreiner and the Anglo-Boer War 1899–1902* (Cape Town and Johannesburg: Human and Rousseau, 1992). A detailed portrait of the war years, drawing on hitherto unpublished sources.

CRITICAL BOOKS, CHAPTERS AND ARTICLES

Barash, Carol, 'Virile Womanhood: Olive Schreiner's Narratives of a Master Race', in *Speaking of Gender*, ed. Elaine Showalter (London: Routledge, 1989), 269–81. Argues that Schreiner's feminism is compromised by colonialist and racist views of white and black motherhood.

Berkmann, Joyce Avrech, *The Healing Imagination of Olive Schreiner: Beyond South African Colonialism* (Amhurst: University of Massachusetts Press, 1989). A richly contexualized discussion of all Schreiner's major works which focuses on her 'integrationist' effort to refuse dualism and opposition in religious, social and political thought.

Bland, Lucy, *Banishing the Beast: English Feminism and Sexual Morality 1885–1914* (Harmondsworth: Penguin, 1995). An excellent historical and analytic account of English sexual politics.

Bradford, Helen, 'Olive Schreiner's "Series of Abortions": Fact, Fiction and Teenage Abortion', *Journal of Southern African Studies*, 21/4 (1995), 623–41. Speculates that Schreiner became pregnant in 1872, and that she repeatedly revisits this theme in disguised forms in her fiction.

Bristow, Joseph, 'Introduction', *The Story of an African Farm* by Olive Schreiner (Oxford: Oxford University Press, 1992), vii–xxxvi. A detailed, well-contextualized account of *SAF*.

Brittain, Vera, *Testament of Youth* (1933; London: Weidenfeld & Nicolson, 2009).

Burdett, Carolyn, *Olive Schreiner and the Progress of Feminism: Evolution, Gender, Empire* (Basingstoke: Palgrave, 2001). Deals with all Schreiner's major work in relation to contemporary intellectual contexts.

Chrisman, Laura, *Rereading the Imperial Romance: British Imperialism and South African Resistance in Haggard, Schreiner, and Plaatje* (Oxford: Oxford University Press, 200), 120–62. Probably the best existing discussion of *TPH*, theoretically sophisticated and densely contextualized.

——, 'Allegory, Feminist Thought and the *Dreams* of Olive Schreiner', *Prose Studies: History, Theory, Criticism*, 13/1 (May 1990), 126–50. An illuminating reading of the allegories as mediating sex, race, and class issues.

——, 'Colonialism and Feminism in Olive Schreiner's 1890s Fiction', *English in Africa*, 20/1 (May 1993), 25–38. Theoretically-informed readings of *TPH* and *DLRL*.

Clayton, Cherry (ed.), *Olive Schreiner* (Johannesburg: McGraw-Hill, 1983). A collection of contemporary reviews, extracts from letters, and critical commentaries from the 1970s and 80s. A valuable and useful resource.

——, Olive Schreiner (New York: Twayne Publishers, 1997). A survey study of Schreiner's life and work, useful and well informed.

Coetzee, J. M., *White Writing: On the Culture of Letters in South Africa* (New Haven and London: Yale University Press, 1988). A collection of essays on white South African writers, particularly insightful about idleness, the pastoral, and the farm novel.

Dinnage, Rosemary, *Alone, Alone! Lives of Some Outsider Women* (New York: NYREV, 2004). Moving reflections of women's experiences of solitariness and isolation. Contains an essay on Schreiner.

Donaldson, Laura E., *Decolonizing Feminisms: Race, Gender, and Empire-Building* (London: Routledge, 1993). Contains a chapter on *FMM*, which reads the novel in relation to theories of the semiotic traffic in women.

Esty, Jed, 'The Colonial Bildungsroman: *The Story of an African Farm* and the Ghost of Goethe', *Victorian Studies*, 49/3 (Spring 2007), 407–30.

Freeman, Hannah, 'Dissolution and Landscape in Olive Schreiner's *The Story of an African Farm*', *English Studies in Africa*, 52/2 (2009), 18–36. Focuses on the representation of Lyndall's body as a mode of fantasy about colonial power.

Gagnier, Regenia, *The Insatiability of Human Wants: Economics and Aesthetics in Market Society* (Chicago: University of Chicago Press, 2000). An influential interpretation of economics and literary culture which contains a reading of Schreiner's WL.

Gilbert, Sandra M. and Susan Gubar, *No Man's Land: The Place of the Woman Writer in the Twentieth Century Vol 1: The War of the Words* (New Haven and London: Yale University Press, 1987). A now classic work of feminist literary criticism which includes discussion of *SAF*.

Gordimer, Nadine, 'Afterword: The Prison-House of Colonialism', in *An Olive Schreiner Reader* ed. Carol Barash (London: Pandora, 1987), 221–8.

Gray, Stephen, *Southern African Literature: An Introduction* (Cape Town: David Philip, 1979). Contains an excellent chapter on 'Schreiner and the Literary Tradition' which focuses on Schreiner as a South African who inaugurates a tradition of white writing.

Gregg, Lyndall (Dot Schreiner), *Memories of Olive Schreiner* (London: W. & R. Chambers, 1957). A memoir by the daughter of Schreiner's brother, Will.

Hackett, Robin, *Sapphic Primitivism: Productions of Race, Class, and Sexuality in Key Works of Modern Fiction* (New Jersey: Rutgers University Press, 2004). Contains a chapter on Schreiner and the late-Victorian New Woman.

Heilmann, Ann, *New Woman Strategies: Sarah Grand, Olive Schreiner, Mona Caird* (Manchester: Manchester University Press, 2004). An influential reading of Schreiner's feminist writing in relation to wider New Woman themes.

Horton, Susan, *Difficult Women, Artful Lives: Olive Schreiner and Isak Dinesen, In and Out of Africa* (Baltimore: Johns Hopkins University Press, 1995). A lively, popular account of the two writers.

Jacobson, Dan, 'Introduction', *The Story of an African Farm* by Olive Schreiner (Harmondsworth: Penguin, 1971), 7–23. Although dismissive of Lyndall's feminism, this gives a powerful account of Schreiner's impact as a South African writer.

Jay, Elisabeth, 'Introduction' to *Dreams: Three Works by Olive Schreiner* ed. Elisabeth Jay (Birmingham: University of Birmingham Press, 2003), ix–xxviii. A useful introduction to Schreiner's short fictions and allegories, collected here (*D.*, *DLRL* and *SDA*).

Jones, Greta, *Social Darwinism and English Thought: The Interaction between Biological and Social Theory* (Sussex: Harvester, 1980). Old, but still very clear and useful introduction to social Darwinism.

Kissack, Mike and Michael Titlestad, 'Olive Schreiner and the Secularization of the Moral Imagination, *English In Africa*, 3/1 (2006), 23–46. Reads the 'Times and Seasons' section of *SAF* and *TPH* in relation to intellectual and emotional currents of secularization.

Knechtel, Ruth, 'Olive Schreiner's Pagan Animism: an Underlying Unity', *English Literature in Transition, 1880-1920*, 53/3 (2010), 259–82. Reads *SAF*, *FMTM* and 'A Dream of Wild Bees' in the context of Schreiner's maternal reworking of Emersonian transcendentalism and Spencerian evolution.

Krebs, Paula M., *Gender, Race, and the Writing of Empire: Public Discourse and the Boer War* (Cambridge: Cambridge University Press, 1999). An excellent history of the politics of representation in relation to the war which contains a chapter on Schreiner's South African writing.

Kucich, John, *Imperial Masochism: British Fiction, Fantasy, and Social Class* (Princeton and Oxford: Princeton University Press, 2007), 86–135. A powerful recent reassessment of Schreiner's work as exemplifying the dynamics of masochistic fantasy. It makes subtle use of psychoanalytic theory in its examination of issues of sexuality, colonialism and class.

Lane, Christopher, *The Burdens of Intimacy: Psychoanalysis and Victorian Masculinity* (Chicago: University of Chicago Press, 1999), 93–118. Chapter on *SAF* focuses on Gregory Rose and sexual difference.

Ledger, Sally, *The New Woman: Fiction and Feminism at the Fin de Siècle* (Manchester: Manchester University Press, 1997). An excellent analysis of the politics of New Woman writing, although critical of Schreiner's perceived social Darwinism.

Lessing, Doris, 'Afterword to Olive Schreiner, *The Story of an African Farm*', in *A Small Personal Voice*, ed. Paul Schlueter (New York: Alfred Knopf, 1974), 97–120. A South African novelist's meditation on Schreiner as a South African writer.

Lewis, Simon, *White Women Writers and their African Invention* (Gainesville: University Press of Florida, 2003).

Livesey, Ruth, *Socialism, Sex, and the Culture of Aestheticism in Britain, 1880–1914* (Oxford: Oxford University Press, 2007). An important recontextualization of Schreiner in relation to 1880s socialism.

Lovell-Smith, Rose, 'Science and Religion in the Feminist Fin-de-Siècle and a New Reading of Olive Schreiner's *From Man to Man*', *Victorian Literature and Culture*, 29/2 (2001), 303–26. An important and illuminating rereading of *FMM* as informed by a distinctive late-century form of feminist polemic which combines science and religion.

Lytton, Constance and Jane Warton, *Prisons and Prisoners: Some Personal Experiences* (London: Heinemann, 1914).

McClintock, Anne, *Imperial Leather: Race, Gender and Sexuality in the Colonial Contest* (New York and London: Routledge, 1995). An influential account of the interrelations between gender, race and class drawing on feminist, post-colonial, psychoanalytic and socialist theories.

McCracken, Scott, 'Stages of Sand and Blood: The Performance of Gendered Subjectivity in Olive Schreiner's Colonial Allegories', in *Rereading Victorian Fiction* eds Alice Jenkins and Juliet John (Basingstoke: Palgrave, 2000), 145–58. Theorized reading of 'Three Dreams in a Desert'.

Monsman, Gerald, *Olive Schreiner's Fiction: Landscape and Power* (New Brunswick: Rutgers University Press, 1991). A detailed literary reading of Schreiner's long and short fiction, paying particular attention to the topographical qualities of her imagery.

Moore-Gilbert, Bart, 'Olive Schreiner's *Story of an African Farm*: Reconciling Feminism and Anti-Imperialism?', *Women: A Cultural Review*, 14/1 (2003), 85–103. A fascinating revision of the conventional assessment of *SAF*'s treatment of race.

Pechey, Graham, '"The Woman's Rose": Olive Schreiner, the Short Story and Grand History', *Critical Survey*, 11, 2 (Summer 1999), 4–17. A moving interpretation of one of Schreiner's stories and its relation to colonial politics and literary praxis.

Porter, Theodore M., *Karl Pearson: The Scientific Life in a Statistical Age* (Princeton: Princeton University Press, 2004). A definitive biography of Pearson which illuminates the idea/ideal of science in the period.

Richardson, Angelique, *Love and Eugenics: Rational Reproduction and the New Woman* (Oxford: Oxford University Press, 2003). The key existing study about how eugenic ideas intersected with New Women writing.

Rowbotham, Sheila, *Edward Carpenter: A Life of Liberty and Love* (London: Verso, 2008). A wonderful biography which includes new material on Schreiner's relations with figures in Carpenter's circle.

Sanders, Mark, 'Towards a Genealogy of Intellectual Life: Olive Schreiner's *The Story of an African Farm*', *Novel: a forum on fiction*, 34, 1 (2000): 77–97. Dense reading of the complex status of intellectual life in *SAF*.

Shiach, Morag, *Modernism, Labour and Selfhood in British Literature and Culture, 1890-1930* (Cambridge: Cambridge University Press, 2004).

Contains a persuasive account of Schreiner's analysis of labour.

Shapple, Deborah L., 'Artful Tales of Origination in Olive Schreiner's *The Story of an African Farm*', *Nineteenth-Century Literature*, 59, 1 (2004), 78–114. Rereads Waldo's association with the 'Bushmen' artists in order to provide a fresh look at the critique of colonialism in *SAF*.

Showalter, Elaine, *A Literature of Their Own: British Women Novelists from Brontë to Lessing* (London: Virago, 1978). A notoriously negative assessment of what Showalter calls the 'feminist' writers of the late-nineteenth century, and of Schreiner in particular.

————, *Sexual Anarchy: Gender and Culture at the Fin de Siècle* (London: Virago, 1992). A more positive assessment of Schreiner, seeing her as central to the sexual, class and race politics of the period.

Stanley, Liz, *Imperialism, Labour and the New Woman: Olive Schreiner's Social Theory* (Durham: sociologypress, 2002). Makes use of unpublished letters, reviews much of the significant Schreiner scholarship, and makes a robust case for her importance as a social and feminist theorist.

————, 'Encountering the Imperial and Colonial Past through Olive Schreiner's *Trooper Peter Halket of Mashonaland*', *Women's Writing*, 7, 2 (2000), 197–219. Useful rereading drawing attention to the complex differentiation between colonial, imperial, and indigenous peoples in South Africa.

Vivan, Itala (ed.), *The Flawed Diamond: Essays on Olive Schreiner* (Sydney: Dangaroo, 1991). Uneven collection deriving from a conference in Verona.

Walkowitz, Judith, *City of Dreadful Delight: Narratives of Sexual Danger in Late-Victorian London* (London: Virago, 1992). Relevant discussions of the Men and Women's Club, and the 'Maiden Tribute' scandal.

Walters, Paul and Jeremy Fogg, 'The Short Sorry Tale of *Trooper Peter Halket of Mashonaland* and its Frontispiece', *English Studies in Africa*, 53, 2 (2010), 86–101. Good historical background and a persuasive account of how Schreiner obtained the frontispiece for *TPH*.

Walters, Paul and Jeremy Fogg (eds), *Olive Schreiner: her Reinterment on Buffelskop* (Grahamstown: National English Literary Museum, 2005). Re-edits the existing account by Cronwright of Schreiner's final burial.

Index

Lightning Source UK Ltd.
Milton Keynes UK
UKOW050844100713

213496UK00001B/11/P